THOMAS HARDY'S
POETRY AND EXISTENTIALISM

THOMAS HARDY'S POETRY AND EXISTENTIALISM

MALLIKARJUN PATIL

ATLANTIC PUBLISHERS AND DISTRIBUTORS

Published by
ATLANTIC PUBLISHERS AND DISTRIBUTORS
B-2, Vishal Enclave, Opp. Rajouri Garden,
New Delhi-110 027
Phones 5413460, 5429987

Sales Office
4346/4C, Ansari Road, Darya Ganj,
New Delhi-110 002
Phones 3273880, 3285873, 3280451
Fax 91-11-3285873
e-mail gupta.atlantc@axcess.net.in

ISBN 81-7156-833-5

Typeset at
APD Computer Graphics, Delhi

Printed in India at
Mehra Offset Press, Delhi

DEDICATED TO

PROF. S.P. HIREMATH

The Hon'ble Vice-Chancellor

KUVEMPU UNIVERSITY, SHIMOGA

BOOK BY THE SAME AUTHOR

1. THOMAS HARDY : THE POET.

Foreward

It is an unmistakable mark of a great writer that he is always our contemporary; that his thought has an urgent relevance to the needs and problems of any time and any clime. Thomas Hardy's work is a shining example of this. Born and bred a Victorian, he thought of life in terms which shocked his contemporaries; today he strikes a chord in every modern heart, for his work is full of intimations of the overpowering sense of crisis and nothingness, alienation and ennui and sisyphian despair, Kurtzian horror and Kafkaesque *angst* which are recurring themes in the literature of our century.

Dr. Mallikarjun Patil's study of Existentialism in the poetry of Hardy is a brave attempt to bring out this vital aspect of the poet's thought. After presenting a lucid account of the origin, growth and development of Existentialism, the author examines the relationship between Man and Nature, Man and Society and Man and his own self in Hardy's poetry, with a view to bringing out similarities between Hardy's thought and Existentialism.

Dr. Patil's study shows close acquaintance with Existentialist thought and thorough familiarity with hardy's poetry. One only wishes he had included hardy's fiction also in his study, for many of Hardy's ideas and predilections expressed emotively in his verse are presented equally effectively in terms of character and situation in his novels.

How often does one wish of an Indian book that it had the benefit of a more efficient editor, who could have saved the author from many manifest infelicities. Surely at this point of Hardy criticism (Dr. Patil's Bibliography itself list more than seventy studies), an entire chapter on Hardy's 'Life and Works' is an obvious redundancy. But Dr. Patil is a young researcher and this is only his second book. One hopes that with more experience and greater maturity, he will produce much better works. His book certainly testifies to a potential which one hopes, will be realized substantially in the years to come.

PROF. M.K. NAIK
Pune

Acknowledgement

It is essential to say a few words about those who have helped me in bringing out this research work. In this regard, I am extremely grateful to Dr. (Smt.) P.N. Rao, the Reader (Retd.), Department of English, Karnatak University, Dharwad who guided me for my Ph.D. on "The Existential Philosophy in Thomas Hardy's Poetry". Not only that, she has inspired me to continue my research in English literature. I am thankful to the Professors of English, Karnatak University, Dharwad, and to my colleagues Department of Studies in English, Gulbarga University, Gulbarga for their suggestions. Finally, I owe an immense debt of gratitude to Prof. M.K. Naik, Prof. S.P. Hiremath and Prof. V.R. Kulli for their suggestions and encouragement and to Dr. K.R. Gupta for the publication of this book and to my wife Dr. Nanda M. Patil for her unstinted co-operation and to my son, Shivakumar and daughters Ashwini, Aishwarya, Shobha and Lalita for their love and affection.

MALLIKARJUN PATIL
Lecturer
Department of Studies in English
Gulbarga University,
Gulbarga-585 106 [India]

A List of Abbreviations used in the Work

WP	—	*Wessex Poems and Other Verses.*
PPP	—	*Poems of the Past and the Present.*
TL	—	*Time's Laughingstocks and Other Verses.*
SC	—	*Satires of Circumstance, Lyrics and Reveries.*
MV	—	*Moments of Vision and Miscellaneous Verses.*
LLE	—	*Late Lyrics and Earlier.*
HS	—	*Human Shows, Far Phantasies, Songs and Trifles.*
WW	—	*Winter Words in Various Moods and Metres.*
Life	—	*The Life of Thomas Hardy* by F.E. Hardy.
Late Years	—	*The Later Years of Thomas Hardy* by F.E. Hardy.
Early Life	—	*The Early Life of Thomas Hardy* by F.E. Hardy.

Introduction

Ever since the rise of literature, there are writers and thinkers par excellence. But writers are not always thinkers. Evidently, Thomas Hardy is one of those writers who like Tolstoi, Sartre and Camus had been both a writer and thinker. However, Hardy has not written any books on philosophy, nor his philosophical ideas are consolidated in a book form, his thoughts are vividly seen in his writings. The poverty in which he was born, his lack of conventional education, his first wife Emma's indifference, London society's snobbery and his invidious critics taught him certain profound experience of life. Consolidating these views Hardy expressed them in his works — poetry, fiction and epic-drama — at various moods and circumstances.

Thomas Hardy's serious or his characteristic double vision of life can be seen in regard to Man, Nature, Society, Religion, God, Fate and Universe. Again Hardy thinks of Man in relation to Nature, Society, his own Self, God, Religion, Fate and Universe. So in his view, Man is central to all these spheres in the stellar Universe which has no regard to human wishes whatsoever.

Right from his boyhood, Hardy studied human life in relationship with Nature, Man in Hardy's view, can live well if he adjusts with his biological surroundings. So 'Man-Nature' relationship found upon equality, love, faith and veneration can be the happiest one. But at times Hardy finds Nature indifferent to human wishes.

What is true of Hardy's views regarding 'Man-Nature' relationship is also true of his views regarding 'Man-Society' relationship. Here we find two levels *i.e.*, 'Man-Woman' and 'Man-Men' relationships. As far the former Man is bound to succeed if he treats his woman with love, fidelity and understanding, while he can live happily in his society only when he enjoys the latter's understanding help and cooperation. In his social environment, an individual is supposed to work properly. In this regard, his service and sacrifice may bring him success and contentment.

However, Man has inherited a Religion, Hardy thinks Religion cannot help him in his hours of crisis. In his view, Religion has lost its organizing and consoling powers. Now it is a spent force. Like Sartre and Kierke-gard, Hardy, an atheist believes man should not depend upon any religion for good or ill. Similar is his existentialistic attitude towards the idea of God. Hardy thinks there is no God. But paradoxical enough, he believes in the existence of a super power calling it Fate. Every literary work Hardy has written displays the fact that this Fate or Destiny at best is never benevolent to human aspirations. More horribly, the Universe in which we live is an embodiment of this Bleak Force and it does not possess any sympathy for human suffering.

It is against this background Man is thrown on this Globe by chance. So his life is an accident. According to Existentialists, man has no prior values or predestination and he has to make his life good or bad in accordance with his acts. Sartre, Camus, Jaspers, Nietzsche — all agree that 'Existence precedes Essence'. Based on this is Heidegger's theory 'Being and Becoming'. In other words, man is nothing but a sum of his acts. None helps him, neither his parents nor any other external forces. In fact, there is no God. So man has to live in harmony with his biological and social surroundings and being in a state of harmony with his innerself, he should work out his own Destiny. No doubt, if he thinks well, chooses rightly, acts accordingly and turns responsible for his misdeeds and improves, he will become a Superman.

The present work *Thomas Hardy's Poetry and Existentialism* analyses the above views of Hardy in the light of Existentialism and makes certain probings quite helpful for the welfare of mankind.

CONTENTS

1

Life and Works of Thomas Hardy

Thomas Hardy, the poet and novelist of the latter part of 19th and the early part of 20th centuries, was born on 2nd June 1840 in a small picturesque cottage built by his grandfather 'Thomas, the first' (1778-1837) in 1801, in Higher Bockhampton, Dorchester, a hundred miles away from London. This Dorchester which later became a region at the heart of Hardy's Wessex and which was covered by the Stinsford parish and the majestic Egdon (Puddletown) heath, was grand in its simplicity and nobility. His father 'Thomas, the second' (1811-1892) and his grandfather 'Thomas, the first' were connected with the profession of architecture. At one time the Hardys had been well-known in Dorset. His epic drama *The Dynasts* (1904-1908) was inspired by his ancestor, the famous Admiral Sir Thomas Masterman Hardy (1769-1839) who had been a captain of Nelson's flagship at the battle of Trafalgar when the latter died. However, the fortunes of the family declined later on account of the later Hardys' laziness. Hardy, the writer, thus brooded over the decline in the fortunes of his family.

His father was a buoyant kindly man passionately fond of music; and he was a violinist and a singer much in demand at village festivities. Hardy's mother, Jemima Hand (1813-1904) was affectionate, cultured and more ambitious than her husband. It was under her care and affection that the boy learnt music and dance before he went to school. She came of a family very fond of reading and she was a systematic and stimulating gentlewoman whose store of memories made remarkable contribution to the upbringing of the boy Thomas. Soon after his dramatic appearance into the world, the boy learnt to read the books offered by his mother. He went to a non-conformist school and learnt Latin and French. As a sensitive boy, Hardy came across many harsh and painful events. He saw a shepherd boy starved to death, a half frozen bird falling dead by his father's stone, ravages of cholera and two public hangings at Dorchester which he remembered the rest of his life. As the boy grew, his parents thought of sending him to Oxford with a view to make him a clergyman. But John Hicks the noted architect and family friend accepted him as a pupil in architectural studies. It was here that Hardy studied diligently many works of great writers in the company of Horace Moule (1832-1873), a Cambridge scholar and William Barnes (1800-1886), a Dorset poet whose works he edited later in 1909.

In 1862 Hardy went to London for studying the art and science of architecture on a more advanced level. It was here that he desired to study for the church, but gave up the idea when he realized that he had no faith in the established religion. He completed the study of architecture under the guidance of Sir Arthur Blomfield (1832-1899) and acquired much knowledge of human existence. Nevertheless, many people considered Hardy a half educated. Like William Shakespeare, Charles Dickens and D.H. Lawrence Hardy did not have any conventional public school and Oxford education, but had read widely and thought more deeply than many highly educated scholars. He was interested in a very wide range of subjects. He knew classical literature, William Shakespeare, the Bible and many of the great English men of letters. By the time he reached London in 1862, he had determined to become a poet, but failed to get acquainted with great poets like Algernon Charles Swinburne (1837-1907) and Robert Browning (1812-1889) who lived close by. He wrote many poems and sent them to magazines but they were rejected. Then he tried his hand at novel-writing simply to earn a livelihood and fame as a writer. Though he lived near Charles Dickens, William Makepeace Thackeray (1811-1863) and George Eliot (1819-1880), he never tried either to meet them or to read their novels. However, he was influenced by poets much more than by novelists. He read William Shakespeare, John Milton (1608-1674) and admired the romantic poets. He has more in common with William Wordsworth (1770-1850) as far as the themes and language of his poems and novels are concerned. He was deeply interested in man's ultimate relationship with the world.

Nevertheless, Hardy was not happy in the capital as he was tired of the sick urban way of life. Therefore, when he got a chance invitation in 1867 from his former master John Hicks from Dorchester, he readily accepted it and returned home.

The first published work of Hardy is neither a novel nor a poem, but an essay *On the Application of Coloured Bricks and Terra Cotta to Modern Architecture* (1864). He sent his first novel *The Poor Man and the Lady* (1868) based on the contrast between city life and village life to Macmillan in vain. Then he decided to get it published at his own cost, but he gave up the idea on the advice of George Meredith (1828-1909) to find his public with a novel of a more complicated plot. It was at this time that he passionately fell in love with his cousin Tryphena Sparks (1851-1890) and considered her his 'lost prize'. His love affair with Tryphena Sparks was intimate and passionate, but he could not marry her. Then he went to St. Juliot near Boscastle in Cornwall to restore a church. It was here, he came to know and love Miss Emma Lavinia Gifford (1840-1912), the sister of the Rector's wife and their marriage took place in 1874 at St. Peter's, Paddington. In the same year, he devoted himself to writing and gave up architecture. Meanwhile, his novel *Desperate Remedies* (1870) had appeared anonymously without any warm reception. *A Pair of Blue Eyes* (1873) which followed *Under the Greenwood Tree* (1871) was admired by Alfred Tennyson (1809-1892) and Coventry Patmore (1823-1896), the leading poets of the day. Similarly, his admirer Sir Leslie Stephen (1832-1904) published his next novel *Far from the Madding Crowd* (1874). Hardy's relationship with Sir Leslie Stephen was more intimate as his second wife Florence Hardy (1879-1937) has noted in her husband's biography.

In the following year 1874, soon after their marriage, the Hardys toured France and then settled down in Sturminster Newton. Here they spent their happiest days untroubled by the disparities of their temperament which later saddened their union. Meanwhile, Hardy got his next novel *The Hand of Ethelberta* (1876) published. He read Joseph Addison (1672-1719), Lord Macaulay (1800-1859), Cardinal Newman (1801-1890), Edward Gibbon (1737-1794) and *The Times* in an effort to polish his style. When Hardy was in search of reputation and decided not to appear merely as a provincial novelist, he received two more requests for new novels. As a result, *The Return of the Native* (1878) and *The Trumpet-Major* (1880) appeared. At the same time, he was asked for short stories. Consequently the best of them collected in *Wessex Tales* (1888), *A Group of Noble Dames* (1891) *Life's Little Ironies* (1894) and *A Changed Man* (1913) were published.

During these years he was worried as he had no issue. Nevertheless, he completed his next novel *A Laodicean* (1881) in great ill health to keep his word to an American editor Harper. After his recovery from an internal hemorrhage, he came to Dorset and built a fine house called Max Gate (1885). It was here that all of his later works were written. A comet which he saw in the year 1882 inspired him to write a slightly built romance *Two on a Tower* (1882). Soon an article appreciating his literary achievements appeared in *Westminster Review*. Immediately his ambitious novel *The Mayor of Casterbridge* (1885) was appeared and it was warmly received on both sides of the Atlantic and his fame and fortune were well established. Similarly, his other novel *The Woodlanders* (1887) was published in the prestigious *Macmillan* magazine.

In the year 1876, the Hardys travelled widely and visited Holland, France, Italy, Belgium and Switzerland. They often stayed in London and befriended many great persons including Edmund Gosse (1845-1928) who became a lifelong friend. During these years, Hardy wrote some essays on fiction *i.e.*, *The Profitable Reading of Fiction* (1887), *Candour in English Fiction* (1889) and *The Science of Fiction* (1891). At the same time he began writing the novel *Tess of the d'Urbervilles* and in the following year (1891) he found it in print. The publication of this novel was followed by many indignant and unreasonable attacks. However, this increased the sale of his novels and brought him fame and fortunes. Wherever Hardy went, Edmund Gosse says, he heard its praise. In fact, *Tess of the D'Urbervilles* took Hardy to the forefront of the living novelists. Moreover, the publication of Lionel Johnson's remarkable critical work *The Art of Thomas Hardy* (1894) consolidated Hardy's stature as an established novelist. Opinions have been divided about Hardy's last novel *Jude the Obscure* (1895) which is a story of two cousins who fall in love with each other but marry the wrong persons. The novel was banned on account of its atheism. According to an American critic it was one of the most objectionable books that Hardy ever wrote. Moreover, Hardy received many mortifying letters which upset him and he became extremely disheartened. This aspect of Hardy's personal crisis is reflected in his poems 'Wessex Heights' (SC) and 'In Tenebris' I and II (PPP). In this state of things perhaps the most painful thing was that his wife Emma instead of consoling him, apparently made her own attempts to stop the publication of the novel *Jude the Obscure*. It is from here that Hardy's tragic years with his wife began. Troubled by Hardy's atheism, rusticity, enquiring spirit and his dislike for the existing marriage and divorce system, she became almost Hardy's enemy. As a result, she began to belittle her husband. In addition to this, social and religious disparities between them added their mite to the rootcause of their internal crisis.

Meanwhile, Hardy published his less popular novel *The Well Beloved* (1896) and in order to forget the publication of his novel *Jude the Obscure*, he went on a tour of the continent. He collected the material for his epic-drama *The Dynasts*. This adventurous work which appeared in three books between the years 1904 and 1908, was received with great respect and acclaim.

After Hardy received severe criticism for his last two novels *Tess* and *Jude*, he turned to poetry for consolation and contentment. His married life that went wrong strengthened his love for poetry. He talked about his novels with contempt, partly because novel-writing was not his true vocation and partly his novels made him unpopular. His first volume of poems *Wessex Poems and Other Verses* came out in 1898, a century after the publication of *Lyrical Ballads*. It was a landmark as it indicated the beginning of modern poetry. However, the publication of *Wessex Poems* surprised the public which had never thought of Hardy as anything but a novelist. Though his poetry was not warmly received by the readers, he decided to continue to write poetry. In this respect, he once told an American professor that he would like to be remembered as poet who had also written some novels. As the years passed by, his stature as a poet was confirmed and his wish to get his poems published in the *Golden Treasury* was fulfilled. While the majority of his novels are criticised, his poems are universally praised. Though many of his poems are neglected by the critics, his reputation as a poet is on the increase in the present century. He became the grand old man or the *doyen* of English letters. But in the year 1912 he was shocked when Emma died of grief and left him in trouble. In this mood of grief and loneliness, Hardy wrote many elegies in memory of her which are included in *Satires of Circumstance, Lyrics and Reveries* under the name "Poems of 1912-13", and are considered to be beautiful. After two years in 1914, in order to restore his domestic felicity, Hardy married his private secretary Florence Emily Dugdale.

During the years of his later life Hardy saw the remaining collections of his poems in print — *Poems of the Past and the Present* (1901), *Time's Laughingstocks and Other Verses* (1909), *Satires of*

Circumstance, Lyrics and Reveries (1914), *Moments of Vision and Miscellaneous Verses* (1917), *Late Lyrics and Earlier* (1922), *Human Shows, Far Phantasies, Songs and Trifles* (1925) and *Winter Words in Various Moods and Metres* (1928) and also a verse play, *The Famous Tragedy of the Queen of Cornwall* (1923).

Hardy was a conscientious writer and worked very hard on his presentation of imagery, diction, prosody and architectonics. His originality, creativity and innovations are really praiseworthy. Even in his old age, he wrote, rewrote, revised and produced new volumes of his poems and novels. When he was 88 years old, his health weakened and he died on 10th January 1928. His burial was witnessed by distinguished writers and great men including the then Prime Minister of England, the Leader of the Opposition, Sir James Barrie (1860-1937), John Galsworthy (1867-1933), Sir Edmund Gosse, Prof. A.E. Housman (1859-1936), Rudyard Kipling (1845-1936) and G.B. Shaw (1856-1950). His ashes were buried in Westminster Abbey in the presence of a great gathering. In the presence of a rural congregation, after a memorial service, his heart was buried in the grave of his first wife Emma Hardy. As a mark of honour to the departed writer, all business ceased for an hour.

Thomas Hardy, the noted poet, novelist, short story writer and an architect was duly honoured by his countrymen. He was a member of Savile Club in 1879; and became a governor of Dorchester Grammar School, a position he held until 1925. He succeeded George Meredith as President of the Society of Authors; and he received Order of Merit in 1910. He received the Gold Medal of the Royal Society of Literature in 1912. He was invited to America many a time, but he rejected the invitations. He received many distinguished awards and honours from several universities. Aberdeen University conferred upon him the degree of LL.D., and he became the president of the society of Dorset men in London. Many players readily staged scenes from his novels and epic-drama. Cambridge University conferred the degree of D. Litt upon him in 1913, the Oxford University in 1920 and the Bristol University in 1925. In 1914 he joined a band of leading writers who pledged themselves to write for the Allied cause. He became the Honorary Fellow of Magdalene College. When the first World War ended, his 78th birthday was celebrated and he was honoured with a specially bound volume of poems and tributes from 50 living poets represented by Siegfried Sassoon (1886-1967). In 1920, when he was made a Fellow of the R.I.B.A, he paid his last visit to London.

Dramatic performances of his works continued and his novel *The Mayor of Casterbridge* was made into a film.

The respect and regard shown to Hardy by the younger men gave him special pleasure during his declining years. 106 of his admirers signed an address to him on his 81st birthday and they expressed the view what would all persons think of him today : "In your novels and poems you have given us a tragic vision of life which is informed by your knowledge of character and relieved by the charity of your humour, and sweetened by your sympathy with human suffering and endurance. We have learned from you that the proud heart can subdue the hardest fate, even in submitting to it.... In all that you have written you have shown the spirit of man, nourished by tradition and sustained by pride, persisting through the defeat."[1]

In a way Hardy may be called a Victorian for he spent the first 60 years of his life in the 19th century which formed many of his beliefs and ideas. However, he is not a typical Victorian as he represents a more modern, adventurous and questioning spirit. He was not only a poet and novelist, but also a versatile genius devoted to architecture, music, painting and even to the problems of modern philosophy. Although he did not formulate any philosophy of his own, his vision of life is revolutionary. He came under the pervasive influence of the scientists and atheist thinkers of Victorian England, especially Charles Darwin (1809-1882), Herbert Spencer (1820-1903), T.H. Huxley (1825-1895), J.S. Mill (1806-1873) and A.C. Swinburne. It was heroic of Hardy that in spite of his loneliness, misery and suffering, he could still carry on. His characteristic double vision of seeing things, both good as well as evil and sublime and silly is noteworthy. In this connection, he was deeply influenced by A.C. Swinburne, an atheist, a poet and a promoter of liberty, and was attracted by his poems 'Hymn to Proserpine' and 'Hymn of Man'. Both Hardy and A.C. Swinburne were existentialists thinking that man has no prior values and he must solve his problems without any external assistance. Hardy's thought underwent a sea change when he came under the spell of the new faith. His conception that there is no God is due to the influence of Herbert Spencer's *First Principles* (1862) and T.H. Huxley's *Agnosticism and Christianity*. Similarly, his view that Nature and society cannot always he benevolent to the existence of an individual is due to the influence of Charles Darwin's *Origin of the Species* (1859) and J.S. Mill's essays. He met both T.H. Huxley and Charles Darwin and he admired them whole heartedly. Hardy saw J.S. Mill once in 1865; he listened to his open air speech; and called him the greatest and most profound thinker of his time. He read his essay *On Liberty* (1859) along with William Wordsworth's poem 'Leech Gatherer' as a cure for his despair. Moreover, his friendship with Horace Moule, William Barnes, Sir Leslie Stephen, Edmund Gosse, Granville Barker (1877-1946) and many others confirmed his enquiry and conviction. Hardy was a serious and earnest writer. His loss of faith in tradition, religion and God led him to think that man had to create his own order of life for an authentic mode of existence in the world which is rather alien to him.

On account of these varied influences, he became a revolutionary youth. It is due to his sweeping critical views on love, marriage, divorce, London society, Christianity and the dogmatic moral and social systems in general that many of his poems and novels were at once sent back by the editors. Hardy was a great humanist and the combination of gentleness and passionate courage made him a unique writer. In politics he was always on the side of public and identified himself with them. He questioned all the common assumptions of his time. In this sense he is a *modern* writer. Hardy preferred to call himself an 'evolutionary meliorist' who believes in the gradual evolution of the world. But out of frustration once he said; "What are my books but one plea against man's inhumanity to man, woman, and the lower animals?.... Whatever may be the interest good or evil of life, it is certain that man makes it much worse than it need be when we have got rid of a thousand remediable ills, it will be time enough to determine whether the ill that is irremediable outweighs the good."[2] This view is clearly reflected in his poem 'In Tenebris' II (PPP). Hardy's bent of mind for abstract speculative thought led him to study Arthur Schopenhauer (1788-1868), Von Hartman (1842-1906) and Haeckel (1834-1919). As a consequence, like A.E. Housman he was called a pessimist and was often considered a gloomy and depressing writer. He was called not only a pessimist, but also a fatalist, non-conformist, agnostic, atheist, and 'churchy' in a strictly non-religious sense. However, Hardy was an optimist and humanist who struggled and excelled in the sphere of human magnanimity and splendour.

Hardy's impact on the younger poets like W.H. Auden (1907-1973) and D.H. Lawrence is great. Like Hardy's novels, D.H. Lawrence's novels were burnt and banned. It is said when *Jude the Obscure* ends, *The Rainbow* begins. Hardy's poetic spirit continued to exist in the works of younger poets like Siegfried Sassoon, Edward Thomas

(1878-1917), Robert Graves (1895-1985) and many others. Even writers like Ezra Pound (1885-1972), Dylan Thomas (1914-1953), C. Day Lewis (1904-1972) and Philip Larkin (1922-1985) have proclaimed their adherence to this "Lord of the Wessex Coast". Indeed, today Hardy is widely read, admired and imitated all over the world.

The answer to the question whether Hardy was a traditionalist or a modern is two fold. The critics of Hardy's time considered him a traditionalist but in a different way. According to them, Hardy followed the tradition both in his life and literature but in a limited way. On the other hand, there are many critics who think that Hardy is a modern. It is on account of his poetic innovations, originality, creativity and architectonics that he is considered a modern. Hardy brought a sea change in the field of versification. Because of his self-study, vast experience and observation of life, Hardy's poetic diction is varied and interesting. He was not simply content to put new wine in old bottles, but he wanted to put new vintage in fresh containers. Hardy's vocabulary is vast and varied. He uses learned words and colloquial expressions. He used archaic, obsolete, rare, poetic, coined and dialect words in order to impart his sense of truth and strangeness. His use of dialect words like, 'garth' (yard), 'leaze' (a grass field), 'moils' (drudgery) etc., like that of his fellow poet William Barnes, adds 'local colour' to his poetry. Similarly, his use of obsolete words like 'collcembrace', 'demilune' (half moon)', 'dorp' (village) etc., and rare words like 'dolesome', 'griff' and 'lacune' etc. are common. For example, in his poem 'The Revisitation' (TL) he uses 'dolesome' instead of 'doleful', 'Griff' to make it rhyme with 'if' and 'Lacune' with 'commune'. There are also some weaknesses. Hardy in his early poetry uses Latin words excessively, but they are rare in his poems written later. Whatever may be the substance of his poems, Hardy generally achieves his best effect by means of monosyllabic diction. The outstanding quality of his diction is its economy and accuracy. For example, Hardy in his poem 'New Year's Eve' indicates the four seasons by four words :

> 'I Have finished another year,' said God,
> 'In grey, green, white, and brown* (231)

Hardy's use of imagery is striking. Whatever may be his source of imagery whether biblical or literary or drawn from his keen observation, it throws valuable light on his inner thought and feeling. The most traditional borrowings of his imagery are connected with life, death,

* These of Hardy's poems are quoted from *Thomas Hardy : The Complete Poems*, edited by James Gibson, Macmillan London, Ltd., 1976.

fate, God, time and universe, and the images of his own are connected with youth, love, marriage and natural world. For instance, he says 'time' runs like the sand in an hour glass. His biblical images bear witness to his familiarity with the Old and New Testaments. For example, he likens the suffering of the protagonists in 'The Stranger's Song' (WP) and 'The Flirt's Tragedy' (TL) to the suffering of Cain. Likewise, the use of 'bond-servants' to characterize mankind; worms in connection with grave and death; and 'mad spinner', 'a pilgrimage' and 'an hour glass' in connection with life is characteristic aspect of his imagery.

The next aspect which counts for his poetic greatness is his prosody, the manner in which he has fused his details that contribute to his stature as a poet. As Hardy is not universally acknowledged as a poet on account of his invidious critics, only a few readers of poetry are aware of the extent of his prosodic experiments. In this regard, James G. Southworth says : "Few know that in the use of the poetic stanza he is one of our most extensive innovators in the modern, or for that matter, any period of our poetry."[3] The critic seems to use the word 'extensive' in a numerical sense. Though Hardy was not a profound experimenter like John Keats (1795-1821) and G.M. Hopkins, he is not a negligible poet. He often uses forms which are appropriate and are in close harmony with the subject matter. For example, the iambic diameter stanza of the poem 'To Lizbie Browne' (PPP) (a^2 b^2 c^2 b^2 c^2 a^2) catches the timid irresolution of the lover. Hardy has done some experiment in prosody even though it is not significant. His craft of versification is diverse and systematic. Every individual stanza stands in such a way that it never mars the poetic unity. Just the same, the substance and form of his poems mingle with each other to produce greater poetic appeal. For example, the weather determines the stanzaic division in the poem, Weathers' :

> This is the weather the cuckoo likes,
> 　　And so do I;
> When showers betumble the chestnut spikes,
> 　　And nestlings fly :
> And the little brown nightingale bills his best,
> And they sit outside at 'The Travellers' Rest',
> And maids come forth sprig-muslin drest,
> And citizens dream of the south and west,
> 　　And so do I. (512)

The time is late spring. Hardy carefully selects the details to make a full, purposive and joyous picture of 'Man-Nature' relationship. James

G. Southworth thinks that nothing disturbs the mood of the poet, not even the showers which only 'betumble'. Liquids abound; the vowels are all front and short; the sibilants, explosives and stops are unvoiced.

Even Hardy's literary notes reveal his care for structure, concern for clarity and economy, balance, repetition, alliteration, crystallizing force and many other details. As James G. Southworth remarks; "He was moving in the right direction and had age not overtaken him and relaxed his powers he might have gone farther than he did."[4] I have taken here a few examples of Hardy's diction, imagery, prosody and architectonic and the nature and scope of my work does not permit a more detailed study. Indeed, my immediate and serious concern is not the way of Hardy's saying the things but what Hardy says about human existence in relation to the biological and material environment and the inner self, and thereafter what Hardy, as a thinker, says about man's self purification, self-preservation and self realization in the light of existentialist ethic.

Hardy is considered a major poet. He has written eight volumes of poems and his stature as a great poet has been increased in the present century. His poetic greatness is not insignificant if it is viewed from the literary and philosophical standpoints. Hardy's poems express his originality of thought, creativity of poetic emotions and innovations in the fields of diction, imagery, prosody and architectonics. Moreover, they evince Hardy's double vision of seeing things both as silly and sublime. Though, his poems do not formulate explicitly any philosophy, they show human existence in the light of existentialist ethic. In this regard, one has to assess Hardy's philosophy of life only after a deep examination of his poems.

REFERENCES

1. Douglas Brown, *Thomas Hardy*, p. 28.
2. Thomas Hardy, qt. by Douglas Brown, *Thomas Hardy*, p. 168.
3. James G. Southworth, *The Poetry of Thomas Hardy*, p. 161.
4. James G. Southworth, p. 195.

2

Existentialism : A Way of Life

Man is nothing but,
A sum of his choice and action,
There is no soul, no religion and no God,
'Man is all in all' of the Universe

Over the years, many men of thought and action have been preoccupied with philosophical studies searching for new ways of life which have resulted in the birth of many philosophical trends. Likewise, the philosophy of existence, even though not in the present form, appeared in 19th century Europe challenging the then existing absolute objective idealism of Hegel (1770-1831).

Actually the origin and development of the philosophy of existence is quite old. In this regard, Socrates (469-399 B.C.), the man of principles who originated the way of thought for human evolution, asserted the need for self-understanding, while Plato (427-347 B.C.) and Aristotle [383 (4) - 322 B.C.] who propounded the theory of 'Being and Becoming' thought that 'Being' was existence and 'Becoming', transcendence. They upheld the view that 'Being' is to be considered always in relation to 'Becoming'. But they said very little about the thread that binds together the various meanings of 'Being' and 'Becoming'. Anyway, the Greek philosophers concluded that 'Being' is a synthesis of 'being' and 'non-being' and 'Becoming' a perpetual transformation of one phase into another.

In medieval times, many scholastic philosophers, almost anti-Aristotelian developed the theory of 'Being and Becoming' which culminated in existentialist ethic in the 19th century. They thought 'Being' is either a collective name of all the individuals or a realm of properties and 'Becoming' a temporal change. Another thinker St. Thomas Aquinas (1225-1274), an Aristotelian, considered 'being' as either a genus or a property, but George Berkeley (1685-1753) rejected this view regarding 'Being' a percipient or the perceived. These thinkers, however, agreed that 'Becoming' is change in time.

In modern times, the views of ancient and medieval philosophers about 'Being and Becoming' have been retained. These philosophers interested in the concrete empirical features of 'Being and Becoming', began to explore psychologically the meaning of 'Being and Becoming'. In this regard, philosophers and psychologists such as George Berkeley, A.N. Whitehead (1861-1947), John Dewey (1859-1952), Benedetto Croce (1866-1952), William James (1824-1910) and Henri Bergson (1859-1941) supported the Aristotelian theory of 'Being' in relation to 'Becoming'. They supported the view that 'Becoming' is closely related to 'Time'. They believed that 'duration' (Time) introduces an element of novelty. But Immanuel Kant (1724-1804) and G.W. Leibniz (1646-1716) rejected this view saying that time flows unrelated to change.

The existentialist thinkers accept the view of Aristotle that 'Being' is existence and 'Becoming' is transcendence. They think that 'Being' and 'Becoming' are inter-related. But they do not accept Aristotle's view of pre-destination which curbs human freedom and responsibility for self-realization. They think that 'Being' is superior as it precedes 'Becoming'. In this connection, they reject Hegelianism which attempts to idealize human existence and adjust it ('Being') to thought ('Becoming'). Instead, as a reaction to this inconsistent conformation, existentialism proposes a subjective interpretation of life and conforms thought to life. In fact, existentialism reverses the old system in order to interpret human existence in the light of subjective will.

The main aim of existentialism is to focus on the problems of human existence with a view to providing solutions. As a result, the leading existentialist thinkers have reinforced the importance of the subjective attitude towards life. They have undermined the importance of objective way of life which either materializes human existence or makes it artificial. That is why the Spanish existentialist thinker, Miguel de Unamuno affirms; "Philosophy is a product of the humanity of each philosopher, and each phiklosopher is a man of flesh and bone who addresses himself to other men of flesh and bone like himself..... He philosophizes not with the reason only, but with the will, with the feelings, with the flesh and with the bones, with the whole soul and with the whole body".[1] Thus, it implies that existentialism is certainly a subjective interpretation of life and it is mainly concerned with human existence in its totality.

Existentialism is not something irrational and absurd or pessimistic and atheistic. It is a new philosophical trend or an attitude which manifested itself in Germany and France to make human existence secure, stable and authentic. Existentialists who revolted against Hegelian idealism, justify the requirement of freedom and responsibility for man to become a free and responsible human being both in his biological and social environments. Existentialism is a philosophy of freedom and responsibility which has beset the people of 20th century in all aspects of its culture and civilization, the private as well as public. It is frightening because it hardly believes in the existence and benevolence of God and it is liberating because it emphasizes on freedom and responsibility for an individual's self-preservation and self-realization.

Broadly speaking existentialism is a subjective interpretation of human life. Although, it appeared as a reaction to the then existing Hegelianism, it renewed human existence in relation to transcendence. It is a way or a philosophy of life which enables every human being to lead an authentic mode of life. In fact, it is an ethic for human action and involvement for self-realization. Karl Jaspers defines existentialism as "the way of thought by means of which man seeks to become himself; .... ."[2] Similarly, Jean Paul Sartre says; "....by existentialism we mean a doctrine which makes human life possible and, in addition, declares that every truth and every action implies a human subjectivity."[3] In this regard, Soren Kierkegaard exhorts man not to follow the dogmatic religious system, while Friedrich Nietzsche thinks that there is 'no ideal, no religion, no soul and no God' and 'man is the master of universe'. Similarly, the later existentialist thinkers uphold the view that human existence should be in relation to transcendence. They think man is nothing but a sum of his choice and action and there is nobody or nothing either to guide him or to alleviate his misery and suffering. Therefore, existentialist thinkers advise man first to know what he should be or become and by what ways and means, then prepare himself for the realization of his aims. Thus, existentialism is a philosophy that confronts the human situations in its totality to know the basic conditions of existence and to establish man's significance emerging out of those conditions.

The basic tenets of the philosophy of existence are right thought, right choice, heroic action and responsibility. On the other hand, it emphasises on atheism, agnosticism and humanism for the full and purposive life of human beings in the purposeless universe. It emphatically insists on man's leading an 'authentic mode of life' which is possible only for man, as he is an emotional, rational and intellectual being. It is apparent from these features that the main aim of exstentialism is to make human existence possible and endurable. In this regard, whatever may be the singular character of the thought of each one of the different thinkers, they all dwell alike upon the question of human existence based on subjectivism.

Existentialist thinkers regard man a unique being, ruled by his passions and driven by his desire for consolation and contentment in the world in which he is placed. According to them, man is free to think and act according to his choice. Here he is not free to breed anarchy and harm the environment and society around him, but he is free to have harmonious co-existence with his community. Moreover, man is responsible for whatever he does in accordance with his flexible nature and preoccupation. He suffers not because of any external forces, but because of his misuse of freedom and responsibility. Moreover, man's future is highly unpredictable, for his nature is largely flexible in the flux and reflux of human actualities. Nevertheless, existentialism as it is solely concerned with the problems of man's life, insists on the transcendence of man with respect to his real life. Hence, it is opposed to objectivism, scientism, solipsism and epistemological idealism. As a whole, it assumes an agnostic position and becomes radical atheism and humanism.

As far as existentialist ethic is concerned, there are two branches, theistic existentialism and atheistic existentialism. The first was developed by the 19th century Danish thinker Soren Kierkegaard (1813-1885). In fact, the term 'existentialism' was coined by him to emphasize the importance of authentic mode of human existence. In this regard, he tried to liberate human existence from the Hegelian idealism. He believed in the existence and benevolence of a divine power, but he did not believe in the benevolence of the religious practices. He says for a better life, man must pursue either 'aesthetic life' devoting himself to art, music and drama, or 'ethical life' seeking happiness in family, business and profession. He advises people to experience life for better understanding. This kind of thought was later developed by the French existentialist thinker Gabriel Marcel (1889-1973) and the German existentialist thinker Karl Jaspers (1883-1969).

The other branch, atheistic existentialism, which is popular today, was propounded by the 19th century German thinker Friedrich Nietzsche (1844-1900). It was later developed by Jean Paul Sartre (1905-1980) and Merleau-Ponty (1908-1961) of France, Martin Heidegger (1889-1976) of Germany, Nicholev Berdyayev (1874-1948) of Russia, J.O. Gasset (1883-1955) and Miguel de Unamuno (1864-1936) of Spain and Nicholas Abbagnana (1901-) of Italy. These thinkers deny the very existence of the two omniscient powers — soul and God which have played an important role in human life in the past. The main reason for their disbelief in these powers is that these two can never be proved by reason. They agree that even thinking about the existence and benevolence of these supreme powers is an expensive hypothesis not worth of further discussion. Hence, they believe that there is only one being, and that is man, a being all in all, and superior to all forms of life.

Whatever may be the divisible forces between the two trends, they take off from a common ground. All thinkers uphold man as the complete master of his biological environment and material world. Man whose existence is a transition from nothingness to transcendence, with the help of his predominant will-power and action, may avail himself of the position of superman. However, his life is inter-related to his biological environment, society and his own inner self. If he works in harmony with his self, society and biological environment and makes right choice and works accordingly, he may attain selfhood. Otherwise, disunited with these respective spheres, he will ruin himself and become a victim (*Dasman or Helot*) of the circumstances.

Though modern man does not believe in the religion-oriented traditional way of life, his close connection with the biological environment (Nature), community (Society) and conscience (Inner self) cannot be denied. In other words, an individual is related to the following three dimensions :

(a) The biological environment (*Umwelt*)

(b) The society (*Mitwelt*)

(c) The inner self (*Eigenwelt*)

As far as man's relationship with the biological environment is concerned, there has been a close bond between man and Nature from time immemorial. The main reason for this is that Nature is all in all, the Creator, the Preserver and the Destroyer of both animate and inanimate objects, including man. Therefore, man has been an intimate part of Nature so much so that it is impossible to consider him as an alien or outsider. He depends on Nature not only for food and shelter, but also for happiness, fulfilment and harmonious co-existence. Moreover, his love of Nature leads him to love of his fellow beings. He loves Nature as he loves his own life; he treats her as mother; and he gains everything from her domain to satisfy his needs. In fact, he cannot live without her support. As a result, she has always been treated as the mother and deity. Indeed, she has been regarded as an embodiment of life.

Though, Man and Nature are indivisible, man, being a rational creature with superior conscience and will-power, has to resolve whether he should be friendly with Nature and achieve self-hood through harmonious co-existence, or remain hostile and be ruined by her malignant forces. In this connection, the most important thing is his attitude towards Nature that either makes or mars his relationship with her as well as his life on this earth. For this reason many philosophers since the time of Aristotle have exhorted man to treat Nature with love and veneration and co-exist with her flora and fauna taking her into confidence. They have also warned man that he must not depend entirely on her for everything, for she is not perfect. According to them, Nature does not have an adequate system which will alleviate human misery and suffering. Aristotle said that Nature is imperfect and blind. Corroborating with this view, Jaspers describes Nature as "....the encompassing Being which is all, and from which all is, it is the total life to which we ourselves belong completely; or Nature is assumed to be the Given, the Other as contrasted to ourselves, it is the unconscious, that which is merely occurring without freedom; without choice".[4] Even Hardy, the poet seems to be of the same opinion.

As far as 'Man-Nature' relationship or Nature's benevolence to human existence is concerned, existentialist thinkers hold different views. Jaspers, a theist, firmly believes in the benevolence of Nature towards the existence of human beings. He states that Nature is an inexhaustible source of food, shelter, happiness, harmony, beauty, bounty, consolation and contentment. According to him, man may get both profit and pleasure from Nature. However, he does not deny the fact, that she is also a destroyer of human existence whenever man opposes her system. Therefore, he emphasizes on man's need to treat Nature as not only a fellow being, but also a friend, a mother and a deity. Subsequently, he assures man the possibility of attaining selfhood if his relationship with her is based on love, veneration, regard, sacrifice, compassion and mutual understanding. In other words, man's relationship with Nature must be ideal and durable. In existentialist ethic, this kind of 'Man-Nature' relationship is called the 'I-Thou' relationship which enables every human being to attain self-realization.

But, in reality the facts of life reveal a different story owing to the advent of science and technology which has mechanized human existence in every sphere of life. On account of science and technology everything is measured in terms of its practical utility and importance. Moreover, human values have been misused or violated on the pretext of social welfare. Similarly, man has become extremely utilitarian and materialistic. As a result, forgetting the real worth of Nature, he has begun a process of exploitation of Nature in order to amass wealth. Consequently, his harmonious co-existence with her has come to an end. Albert Camus (1913-1960), French thinker and writer, affirms this view, when he thinks that modern man, by destroying Nature, has deprived himself of the means of meditation; for, "When Nature ceases to be an object of contemplation and admiration, it can be nothing more than material for an action which aims at transferring it".[5]

Man's mastery and control over the biological environment is not bad in itself, if it is utilized judiciously for the mutual uplift of both man and Nature. In fact, his knowledge of the biological sphere must be properly used to enhance and enrich his relationship with Nature. On the contrary, industrialization, urbanization, and commercialization have disturbed 'Man-Nature' relationship in every respect. Therefore, existentialist thinkers criticise the misuse of science in every walk of life. Heidegger hates science "... for being founded on presuppositions, for leaving existence out of consideration, for being based on the subject-object opposition, and for operating with a system of pure representation".[6] Man's extreme attachment to science has made even his instruments alien to her. There is no sign of reconciliation between them at present.

As opposed to the positive view of Jaspers about the implicit benevolence of Nature to the existence of human beings, almost a negative view is propounded by Sartre and Nietzsche. Sartre, the leader of atheistic existentialism, rejects Jaspers' view that Nature is not hostile to man unless he is hostile to her. On the contrary, he considers Nature as not only neutral, but also indifferent to human existence. It is indifferent in the sense that Nature is blind to and unconscious of the misery and suffering of human beings. To Sartre,

Nature appears to be nothing more than a mine of scattered wealth and "disorganized masses"[7] of the purposeless universe. According to him, man's relationship with Nature is characterized as absurd, a mere illusion; "Absurd, irreducible : nothing, not even some secret deep-down madness in nature could explain it".[8] All natural phenomena, including the flora and fauna and the elements seem to be a mute mass of biological and cosmic objects. Nietzsche supports Sartre when he remarks that the biologists have to rear strong individuals instead of working on the evolution of new species. These thinkers often bother about the natural calamities like flood, drought and storm which overshadow the positive aspects of life by their poignancy and horror. Indeed, in the advent of science and technology, the wealth of Nature appears to them either a mere illusion or a mute mass of biological environment. Following this hypothesis, Sartre rejects Japsers' view that there is a possibility of establishing harmonious relationship between man and Nature. He thinks that 'Man-Nature' relationship is highly impossible as Nature is not only neutral but also indifferent and malignant to human misery and suffering. According to Sartre, Nature is imperfect and lacks a coherent system of its own. This aspect of Nature's imperfection, neutralism and malevolence has been recognized by many thinkers since the time of the great Greeks. As already mentioned, it is Aristotle who first exhorted man not to depend on Nature for everything since she is imperfect. Sartre too denies the possibility of a congenial 'Man-Nature' relationship.

Subsequently, man either because of his non-adjustment with Nature on account of his interest in the promotion of science and technology or because of Nature's malevolence on account of her lack of an adequate system, alienates himself from her and seeks consolation and contentment in his own community.

Man's painful alienation from the meditative and benevolent Nature deprives him of a natural harmonious life. As a result, he remains in a state of unrest, ambiguity, dread and disappointment.

Man after his active detachment from Nature turns to his fellow-beings for consolation and contentment. For this he seeks adjustment and reconciliation with his neighbours. In order to establish a peaceful and productive social relationship, an individual loves and respects his neighbours; he understands and trusts them; and finally he sacrifices something for the welfare of his fellow-beings. He also devises various means and ways of harmonizing his relationship with society. In fact, he tries to establish a cordial social order of life based on the virtues of 'equality', 'liberty' and 'fraternity'.

Existentialist thinkers like Jaspers and Ponty regard man's relationship with society as indispensable. They accept man's unsteady and unpredictable nature, but they reinforce the necessity of human desire for mutual understanding and co-operation. They emphasize the need for sublime virtues like love, sympathy and sacrifice in man to establish a harmonious interpersonal relationship. According to them, man must be aware of the world which he immediately and intuitively discovers and experiences, and must be conscious of his existence in point of space and time. Following this, they believe that the relationship between an individual and society is usually successful barring some conflicts. Anyway, man's relationship with others, either ill or well, is an essential phenomenon, and without it an individual's existence is bound to end in conflict or failure. Therefore, Ponty remarks; "We are involved in the world and with others in an inextricable tangle".[9] Man is in society because he finds himself among other people; and he is in the world because he is surrounded by the biological and material environments. Similarly, Heidegger considers this state of man's involvement in society, an essential phenomenon. Likewise, Jaspers who does not believe in Sartre's absolute ethical isolation, declares; "Being-there (the objective world known by observation and experiment), Being-oneself (the personal existence of one who is awakened to his liberty and assumes his historicity and affirms himself in decision and choice), Being-in-itself (the transcendence of the world, manifested in the world and inseparable from it), these three realms of Being are in no sense reducible to one another".[10] These three spheres, the subjective 'I', the objective 'world' and the transcending 'society' are inseparable from one another. Jaspers calls this mode of inter-relationship as 'Communication' established for the sake of harmonious co-existence of human beings. Though Sartre clung to his idea of absolute isolation, he clearly states that man cannot live alone. According to him, 'Being-in-itself' (the world), 'Being-for-others' (society) and 'Being-for-itself' (the man or nothingness) all constitute the concept of existence. He does not deny the need of society for the ascendence of man in his social setting. Like Jaspers, he thinks that man has to unite with others in such a way as to stand in life wrestling with his difficulties. Indeed, "In order to bring in a greater element of control over his affairs man unites with others to form a group".[11] In this connection, one thing must be remembered and that is man's life with others involves the concept of responsibility. Sartre's idea of responsibility as detailed in his work *Existentialism* (L' *Existentialism est un Humanisme* 1947), is two-fold. Firstly, an individual must be responsible for the authentic existence of 'himself' and his or her 'respective spouse', and secondly, he or she has to be responsible for the welfare of 'others' (society). However, in the former a person is closer and more intimate, whereas, in the latter, a person is just a detached observer as a member of the society.

According to Jaspers, man's relationship both with his respective 'spouse' and 'community' will be harmonious and endurable, if it is based on love, compassion, willingness, fidelity, brotherhood, equality, reciprocity, understanding, adjustment and a spirit of sacrifice. Otherwise, 'Man-Woman' or 'Man-Society' relationship is based on enmity, cruelty, jealousy, selfishness, indifference, mistrust and misunderstanding, it will certainly end in man's alienation from others, instead of leading to his self-realization. As a result, such an individual will be deprived of his freedom in society. Therefore, Kierkegaard asserts; "The task is not to exalt the one at the expense of the other, but to give them an equal status, to unify them in simultaneity; the medium in which they are unified is existence".[12] The relationship with others in requisite for one's freedom which depends entirely on the freedom of others. Sartre thinks if man is aware of himself he is also aware of others and others are as important as himself. If he understands himself wholly and thoroughly, he can understand others well. He observes; "In order to get any truth about myself, I must have contact with another person. The other is indispensable to my own existence, as well as to my knowledge about myself. This being so, in discovering my inner being I discover the other person at the same time. This is the world in which man decides what he is and what others are."[13]

Even in sexual relationship the virtues of love, veneration, equality, co-operation and sacrifice become indispensable for higher co-ordination between man and woman. Hardy supports this view when he says; "Love withers under constraint : its very essence is liberty; it is compatible neither with obedience, jealousy, nor fear....A husband and wife ought to continue united only so long as they love each other."[14] As great love deserves sacrifice either on the part of one or the other, human relationship is possible and successful only in the context of absolute love, fidelity, respect, mutuality and willingness.

That is why, intrigues, hostility, self-deception and pretenses must be avoided in 'Man-Woman' relationship.

Similarly, inter-personal relationship on the broader level in society must also be based on equality, liberty, fraternity, sacrifice, mutual respect and genuine understanding. Otherwise, 'Man-Society' relationship will deteriorate and end in man's alienation from society.

On the whole, existentialist thinkers, led by Jaspers, conclude that man may succeed in his attainment of selfhood, if he is capable of adjusting, readjusting and reconciling with his respective 'spouse' as well as 'society'. They also believe that since man is a social animal, the harmonious relationships both between 'Man and Woman' and 'Man and Society' will be possible and successful.

On the other hand, Sartre takes the issue too far. He emphatically states that man's relationship with his respective 'spouse' as well as 'society' will hardly be successful on account of man's flexible nature and unpredictable future. According to him, man's vices, shams, pretences, unworthy aspirations and self deception on account of his growing desire to lead comfortable life, to amass wealth and to dominate others, certainly crush his interrelationships in both dimensions i.e., man's relationship with woman as well as man's relationship with society. Man's inner greed, ambition, avarice, enmity, disbelief, disregard and misunderstanding surely degenerate his way of life and style of functioning. For instance, on account of man's greed, the prevailing systems of 'prostitution' and 'slavery' show the glaring failure of 'Man-Woman' and 'Man-Society' relationship respectively. In existentialist ethic, this kind of inhuman relationship is characterized by the term 'I-It'.

According to Sartre, as far as 'Man-Woman' relationship is concerned, the most serious factor in destroying love is the lover's or wedded person's greed for 'possession'. As the human virtues like equality and mutual understanding are violated or misused, the relationship between man and woman ends in sexual exploitation and seduction as it is clearly seen in prostitution. Thence, such a broken relationship ends either in conflict or in mutual destruction. Both, Sartre and Kierkegaard are of the same opinion as far as seduction and sexual exploitation of woman is concerned which according to them is the result of man's sexual compulsion. In this context, they say, man always desires other women, while woman always clings to one man, for Nature makes her intuitively and consciously care and pursue a supporter and protector of her future off-spring. Sartre thinks 'Man-Society' relationship hardly succeeds on account of one or another's desire for domination. The reason for this crisis, Sartre believes is that 'I' is primary and more important than the secondary 'Thou' as 'existence precedes essence'. Consequently, to an existing individual, the other seems less important than 'I' the self. This devaluation of the other causes disaster in human relationships. Hence, an individual alienates himself from the 'society' as "Man is in absolute ethical isolation and totally responsible"[15] to himself to do whatever he thinks fit for an authentic mode of life. Therefore, Sartre says, harmonious 'Man-Woman' relationship is impossible on account of man's desire to be free from an 'arrested mode of life' or 'lostness in the crowd'. So he closely reaffirms; "As far as I am concerned, another person is no longer a representation of another person; he is a subtilized object."[16] This leads him to say that one's freedom (society's domination) is another's (an individual's) doom. To avoid this doom (sexual and social crises) Sartre prefers alienation and life in isolation. On account of this social anarchy, many existentialist thinkers express their contempt for the society which hinders the way of individuals to prosper. They think 'man is kind but men (society) are cruel'. Kierkegaard speaks contemptuously of society by describing it as 'crowd' and 'trampling geese'. He affirms that it is always the individual versus the crowd and the crowd is the greater destroyer. According to him; "A crowd not this crowd or that, the crowd now living or the crowd long deceased, a crowd of humble people or of superior people, of rich or of poor, etc. — a crowd in its very concept is the untruth, by reason of the fact that it renders the individual completely impenitent and irresponsible, or at least weakens his sense of responsibility by reducing it to a fraction."[17] Indeed, crowd is merciless, malignant and irresponsible, hence it is not a company. This aspect is also evident in the works of Shakespeare, Sartre, Camus and Kafka. Nietzsche who does not distinguish an individual from the society, but makes a distinction between 'village folk' and 'city people' advocates man, the virtues such as simplicity, sincerity, nobility, novelty, hardwork, determination and straightforwardness for his progressive enlightenment in society. He is also anxious about the future of interpersonal relationship owing to the advent of science and technology. Therefore, he remarks that our scientifically minded age, in losing its living faith in sublime virtues, is on the verge of complete extinction.

So these thinkers, Sartre, Kiekegaard and Nietzsche uphold almost a negative view of 'Man-Society' relationship. They vehemently conclude that in the pride of power, prestige and fortune all personal and social relationships are bound to fail and end in man's ethical alienation from society.

Man after his estrangement from society stands in solitude as a forlorn consciousness striving for higher phases of life. His goal to exalt and become superman is temporarily hampered by his inevitable abandonment of the society. In this Crusoe-like existence, he is only counterbalanced by his patience, superior consciousness and intelligence. In this circumstance, Sartre asserts that man's life will be a success or a failure according to his quality of conscience, choice and subsequent action. Though, like Kierkegaard, Sartre does not give importance to inner reality for man's self-purification, he states man must be courageous and confident for his future. The growth of conscience, heroic action and responsibility are essential for man's self-preservation and self-realization. Human consciousness is a key to the knowledge of biological environment and material world. In fact, as the Indian philosopher, Sri Aurobindo thinks the world can only be deciphered by consciousness. Even the Indian schools of philosophy *Dvaita, Advaita* and *Nyaya Vaisesika* emphasize 'consciousness' (*cit* = awareness) for 'being' (*sat* = existence) and 'becoming' (*jnan*-essence). They consider consciousness as something born out of meditation of the soul. But many existentialist thinkers do not believe in this concept as they disbelieve in the very existence of soul. On the other hand, in Western philosophy the Kantian subjective legacy of regarding consciousness as creative of reality has been accepted by existentialist thinkers. Similarly, Hardy thinks consciousness is the main power for 'being and becoming'. Like Ralph Waldo Emerson (1803-1882) and Henry David Thoreau (1817-1862), the American transcendentalists, he thinks that mind is a transcendental force and it is a pure intentional activity for transcendence, but not transcendence in itself. Moreover, Hardy like Sartre, states that self-consciousness must be the very being of the mind in action. Even Heidegger maintains the same when he thinks that consciousness is the starting point of existence". Accordingly there can be no consciousness unrelated to the 'world', and no 'world' unrelated to consciousness, and the two together constitute a bi-une-reality which we call human existence."[18] Above all, consciousness is not an alien faculty. It is inseparable from man. It is both knowing and living. So it remembers the 'historicity', anticipates the 'future' and engages itself in the 'present'. Nevertheless, man cannot live only by his consciousness good or bad, he needs authentic mode of life and style of functioning. He lives only when his inward consciousness and outward actions are coherently related and worked together. In this respect, the subjective way of life is more beneficial as man gets inspiration and encouragement by his emotions and feelings which are more powerful. As a result, man's attachment with reason is curtailed in the philosophy of existentialism. Nietzsche aptly puts it thus; "Destroying the passions and carvings, merely as a preventive measure against their stupidity and unpleasant consequences....(is) an acute form of stupidity."[19] Man's instinctual passions which constitute life and inspire actions are fundamental for human existence. In R.A. Sinari's words "The becoming of an existent is nothing but the manifestation of a passion to live and live infinitely. 'It is impossible to exist without passion'."[20] It is true that emotion is the motive power of human activities. Oscar Wilde (1856-1900), the exponent of aesthetics thinks that great emotions give us quickened sense of life, but the growth of reason dries up the source of creative life. The most enduring things in the world of growth and change are the human emotions and passions. It is also observed that most of the miseries of mankind stem from the suppression of passions. Another thinker, Jean Wahl affirms; ".....existence is *becoming*. Passion and decision are movements. Existence is not definable, but by calling it a movement, a becoming, we characterize it legitimately, for we define it in terms of temporality, continuous becoming, a task....; it is not a logical becoming, but one that grows out of choices and decisions made in the heat of passion."[21] Hardy the poet also gives much importance to the emotional aspects of human existence when he says; "Poetry is emotion put into measure."[22] With this passionate state of consciousness and mental tension, an alienated man remains in a state of *angst* (Kierkegaard), dread (Heidegger), 'anguish' (Sartre), 'anxiety' (Nietzsche) and 'nothingness' (Hardy). As the bereft man's consciousness weakens, his loneliness, ambiguity, despair and anguish grow to such an extent that finally he is led to psychic tumults and tensions. This is because of his clash and conflict between his 'inner conscience' (*cit* = awareness) and 'outer commitments' (*kriti* = action). Consequently, this state of human existence leads to 'self-alienation' (*vinash* = destruction).

In recent years, existentialism has concentrated its attention on the problem of alienation, which has various implications. It includes an extraordinary variety of psychosocial disorders like ambiguity, dread, despair, anxiety, loneliness, nothingness, isolation, pessimism, atheism, absurdism, loss of faith and selfhood, rootlessness and meaninglessness. Kierkegaard, the founder of the philosophy of existence does not differ much from the view of traditional thinkers. But he emphasizes the need for alienation to restore human destiny and individuality. However, his follower Marcel supports him saying that alienation is necessary to man to exercise his freedom of choice and action. Similarly, Heidegger and Sartre state that man's existence in the world is fundamentally with others, but active attachment of an individual to others will be 'an arrested mode of existence' or 'lostness in a crowd'. According to them, man's 'arrested mode of existence' results in his inauthentic mode of existence and loss of identity or individuality. Marcel and Buber who do not agree with Sartre's idea of freedom that 'man is condemned to be free', opine that man must alienate himself from his biological environment and society only to make a better use of freedom and responsibility for the attainment of selfhood. In this regard, the way they recommend is 'stoic-resignation'. Berdyaev, the Russian existentialist thinker also supports the view that psychic isolation or alienation is amply rewarding for it opens the gateway of truth and authenticity. He asserts that man can be or become aware of his personality, originality, singularity and uniqueness from the rest, only when he is free and alone. Indeed, man's alienation from Nature and Society at the psychological level has been considered fruitful in the philosophy of Marcel, Heidegger, Sartre, Buber and Berdyaev.

However, the characteristic feature of existentialism is that man's separation from his biological environment, society and his own self is to establish some universal form of justification which will enable him to readjust himself with the actualities of life. Nevertheless, the lone man whose existence after his inevitable alienation from Nature, Society and his own Self is considered insignificant in society, is counterbalanced by his growth of superior conscience, will-power, heroic action and responsibility. Similarly, man even in his trials and tribulations of life achieves self-realization. Consequently, the existence of such a liberated and self-reliant man is hailed as an authentic mode of existence, and his existence is considered as the personification of the will to power or superman's existence.

It is true the process of 'becoming' is more important and essential than 'being' to an individual who is in quest of selfhood. Albert Camus thinking that man should go on achieving something even in the face of his alienation and absurdity, observes thus; "...the true greatness is for a certain if man is to fight today for grandeur in despair."[23] Therefore, like Nietzsche, he advocates man to create his own order of life and exalt and elevate his existence amidst the face of glaring misfortunes. In a similar spirit Sartre affirms; "Man is nothing else than his plan; he exists only to the extent that he fulfills himself; he is therefore nothing else than the ensemble of his acts, nothing else than his life."[24]

After man's estrangement from his biological environment, material world and inner self, the necessary ingredients of human existence such as conscience, choice, freedom, action and responsibility which often go together, play an important role in the course of man's self-projection, self-preservation and self-realization. These virtues are, in fact, interrelated, for there is no decision without 'thought', no choice without 'decision', no action without 'choice' no responsibility without 'action' and none of these without 'freedom'. Here 'freedom' which is all in all, is identified with choice, awareness and selfhood. Indeed, to choose means to be free and man's freedom is his existence in relation to transcendence. However, the significance of heroic action for man's escape from rootlessness to self realization is never denied in existentialist ethic. That is why Jaspers states; "Freedom is experienced as both spontaneity and action; it is thus more important to act and be an *homme engage* than to observe and be a theoretician."[25] Here man is nothing but his choice and action. Yes, 'he is a sum of his total acts' (Sartre), 'the novelist of himself' (O.Y. Gasset) and 'his own master' (Hardy) who makes promises, determines his future and accordingly shapes it.

Man has no prior values like thought and destiny but only existence and attainment of essence. "Existence 'does not come within the province of thought to think'; above all, thought is not superior to nor a substitute for existence."[26] So thought is secondary, instrumental and subordinate. Sharing this view, Nietzsche asserts that until then only values assessed that personality of a human being, but now a human being taking on himself the full burden of freedom and responsibility, raises himself to the mode of atheistic and authentic existence. If man does this, Nietzsche thinks, he will not only conquer God, but also conquer nothingness. Indeed, existence is higher than thought in which "one should be prepared to raise above the 'herd' and be 'exceptional' and individualistic for the sake of the truth to which he is committed."[27] However, existentialist thinkers deny man any help either from God or religion. They also disbelieve in the absolute benevolence of Nature and Society. They reject the dogmatic conceptions like fate, superstition and witchery. According to them, "No one *gives* man his qualities neither God, nor society, nor his parents and ancestors."[28] Hence, "Man is man's future."[29] He is nothing other than a sum of his acts. Consequently, "One can win the great triumph only if one is true to himself."[30]

Now the question is who is the authentic existent in the new order of human society? The most modest answer is this the man who is most sublime in his virtues and withstands a maximum amount of difficulties; and the man who is heroic in actions and responsible to his commitments good or bad — such a man is a hero, the strongest authentic man of mankind. No doubt, it is true what the Mughul king Babur (1484-1530) thinks; "The world is his who exerts himself"[31] and it is also true what the Norweigian dramatist Henrik Ibsen (1826-1906) observes; "The strongest man in the world is he who stands most alone."[32] Indeed, "The man who can really stand alone in the world, only taking counsel from his conscience — that man is a hero."[33] The philosophy of existence is similar to Buddhism. It is a philosophy of action and involvement and there is no place for *Dasman* or *Helot*. People may sympathize with such a man but they are not likely to care for him or console him. On the other hand, the exalted and elevated individual is hailed a Superman.

Existentialism in Literature

After World War I, the existentialist attitude spread and grew everywhere for man's quest to secure a stable and harmonious human existence. This new phase produced a great galaxy of existentialist philosophers, thinkers and writers like Soren Kiekegaard in Denmark, J.P. Sartre, Gabriel Marcel, Albert Camus and Merleau Ponty in France, Friedrich Nietzsche, Karl Jaspers, Martin Heidegger and Jean Wahl in Germany, Nikolai Berdyaev in Russia, Ortega Y Gasset Jose and Martin Buber in Spain and Nicholas Abbagnano in Italy. Similarly, literary writers like Franz Kafka, Andre Gide, Thomas Hardy, Graham Greene (1904-19991), Iris Murdoch (1919 –), Samuel Beckett (1906–), Nae Ionesco (1890-1940) and Norman Mailer (1923 –) are all in a sense existentialist writers.

The philosophical as well as literary works of these great men reflect one or another aspect of existentialism. Sartre's works such as

Nausea (1938) and *The Flies* (1947), Nietzsche's *Thus Spoke Zarathustra* (1892), Heidegger's *Being and Time* (1927) and Jaspers' *Man in the Modern Age* (1932) and the literary as well as philosophical works of Beckett, Ionesco, Greene, Kafka, Murdoch, Camus and Hardy are enough to understand and assess the impact of existentialism on literature in the present century. On the other hand, the works of Kierkegaard and Nietzsche show deep influence of existentialism in theology.

Though the philosophy of existence seems to be quite modern, it can be traced back to Blaise Pascal (1623-1662), St. Augustine (354-430) and even to Socrates. But it was fully developed in the 19th and 20th centuries. Its immediate sources are the philosophy of St. Augustine and Lord Buddha (566-486 B.C.), phenomenology of Edmund Husserl (1859-1938) and the doctrines like 'equality', 'liberty' and 'fraternity' of the French Revolution (1789). However, it suddenly appeared in 19th century as a reaction to the Hegelian idealism and the materialism prevalent in European thought.

The philosophy of existence spread everywhere in the fields of science, social reform, politics and literature. In the field of literature, writers whether theists or atheists, began to think on new lines. Writers and thinkers alike in Europe hoped to create a new order of life in the then existing systems. Nietzsche, Tolstoy, Bentham, Mill and many others, reacting against the traditional way of life, upheld the view that human life must be changeable and adjustable according to the needs of man's existence. Kierkegaard severely reacted both against Hegelianism and traditional religion. Similarly, Nietzsche announced the death of God and asserted that religion is a bundle of dogmas and rituals. The thoughts of these two thinkers were developed by later existentialist thinkers such as Sartre, Jaspers, Heidegger, Marcel, Buber and others. These thinkers gave a strong jolt to the orthodox religion, the concept of God, benevolence of Nature, Society and the traditional way of life. Similarly, in the field of social reforms and politics, Jeremy Bentham, the father of utilitarianism, pleaded for the greater good of the greatest number. He and his followers, like Rousseau, believed and preached absolute freedom for the individual. J.S. Mill, the great social reformer of Victorian England taught people the importance of individual liberty. Mill was also a great believer in the equality of sex, and his advocacy of the cause of women led to a better appreciation of their status in society. In a similar spirit, many scientists brought revolutionary changes. Lyell's works on Geology

(1830-1863) established the fact that the earth was millions of years old, and man too had lived on earth for a much longer period than that given in the Bible. Darwin's monumental work *Origin of the Species* (1859) and *Descent of Man* (1871) related man to the lower forms of life and demonstrated with evidence that man has descended from the ape. The discoveries of science agitated man's mind and brought a new perception of human existence.

However, the influence of existential philosophy is greater in the field of literature. Almost all writers all over the world directly or indirectly came under the influence of the basic tenets of existentialism. People in modern time, regardless of their interest in literature, philosophy or theology realized the fact that God is indifferent to the misery and suffering of human beings. Even some people thought that there was no God and man was all in all in the universe. They also thought that religion which was mixed with dogmas was defective. Consequently, they concluded that because of God's malevolence and defective religion, man's existence in society was difficult. They expressed the view that owing to his limitations and social codes man could not lead a harmonious existence.

Nevertheless, the possibility of a happy and harmonious human existence is never denied in the philosophy of existence. A close inspection of the works of Camus, Kafka, Gide, Sartre, Berdyaev, Hardy, Greene, Murdoch, Beckett, Mailer and Ionesco reveals the fact that man must be self-conscious or be aware of his sense of duty, limit of freedom and responsibility to attain self-realization :

> Self reverence, self-knowledge, self-control,
> These three alone lead to sovereign power.

Similarly, another Victorian poet, A.C. Swinburne expresses the views which are opposed to the traditional way of life, religion and God :

> By the name that in hell-fire was written, and burned at
> the point of thy sword,
> Thou art smitten, thou God, thou art smitten; thy death
> is upon thee, O Lord.
> And the love-song of earth as thou diest resounds through
> the wind of her wings —
> Glory to Man in the highest ! For Man is the master of
> things.

The philosophy of existence is also evident in modern fiction. The novels of Charles Dickens, George Meredith, George Eliot, Graham

Greene, Thomas Hardy reveal the impact of existentialism on fiction. As we know, Dickens in his novels, depicts an individual's struggle for existence and his relationship with his environment and society. He exposes the evils of moral and social order in the life of his times. His novels like *Hard Times*, *Bleak House*, *Great Expectations* and others are a scathing criticism of life of his age. Similarly, George Eliot, George Meredith, Thomas Hardy and many other modern novelists have dealt with different aspects of existentialist ethic. They have pictured the lives of their heroes in the light of existentialism.

The main idea of these writers is that if man lives in perfect harmony with his biological environment, society and his inner self, he may attain whatever he best deserves. If he wills otherwise, his life ends in self-alienation. For instance, in the works of existentialist thinkers like Sartre, Camus, Kafka and Dostoyevksy, one may clearly see, how an individual tries to establish a new order of life and why he often fails in his mission due to his limitations and social codes. In Sartre's novel *Nausea*, the hero Roquention tries to adjust with society. But when he finds it difficult for him to co-exist with society, he alienates himself from it. Similarly, in Kafka's novel *The Trial*, the hero Josef K suffers due to the erratic system of government. Likewise, in Camus and Dostoevsky's novels, one may explicitly find a clash and conflict between an individual and society for the establishment of supremacy.

In the works of modern writers, a clear diffusion of existentialist ethic is evident. Almost all writers, who directly or indirectly are aware of the importance of existential philosophy, have expressed their views on Man, Nature, and Society, and their relationship with one another on the one hand, and God, Religion and the moral and social order of life and their relation to man on the other. They have pictured man's life in his fortunes and misfortunes with a view to delineate man's struggle for existence in a new perspective. The philosophy of existence is similar to that of Romanticism and if is the basis of modern theatre of absurd. It is similar to the first as far as its emphasis on man's emotional aspects of existence is concerned. Existentialism, like Romanticism, restores man his dignity as a human being. It marks the most important stage in the history of human self-consciousness. It introduces a subjective way of life in which an individual in his own depths continues to be himself and fulfils his destiny. Though it is a subjective way of life, it enables every human being to attain truth, power and glory.

Existentialism is closely associated with the theatre of absurd as far as its typical doctrines like novelty, agnosticism, atheism, optimism and pessimism are concerned. Above all, the traits like right thought, right choice, heroic action and responsibility, dread, ambiguity, atheism and a feeling of nothingness highlight the distinguishing marks of existentialist ethic.

The existentialist writers and thinkers are mainly realists. They write about man's struggle for existence in relation to his progressive enlightenment and transcendence. They devise various means and ways for the liberation of human existence from the fetters of past. They defy the authority and tradition for the attainment of truth and justice. It is on account of their radicalism and humanism the communists accused them as irrationalists neglecting the gracious and beautiful aspects of human existence. But in reality, it is not true that existentialism deals with the ugly aspects of life, as it advocates the ideal philosophy of life to live and let others live. Though outwardly it seems frightening, it is a philosophy of liberation from the shackles of materialism and religion-oriented traditional way of life. Indeed, existentialism enables every human being to perfect his self-hood.

The common themes of existentialism are freedom, choice, decision, action, responsibility, atheism, agnosticism and dread. It is because of these themes many people accuse existentialism of radicalism, violence and non-conformity. Furthermore, many people associate existentialism with the merely atheistic and pessimistic literature of our time. It is true that existentialist literature is mainly atheistic as it is concerned with the practical problems of human existence. It is certainly a philosophy with a purpose. The philosophy of existence is an ethic and involvement for human progress, evolution and enlightenment.

Existentialism and Thomas Hardy

On a closer observation of Hardy's life and achievements, it becomes clear that Hardy's views are quite similar to that of the existentialist ethic. His ethic and involvement is not much different from that of Kierkegaard and Nietzsche, his contemporaries, and Jaspers, Heidegger, Sartre and Camus, his junior contemporaries who were existentialist thinkers as well as writers.

Thomas Hardy was born and brought up in the 19th century England. Though many of his beliefs and ideas were formed in the

Victorian times, his outlook was quite modern. He lived, thought and wrote not only as an observer but also as an active participant in the modern world of science and commerce. Though many ideas of existentialism were in the air and were not known to him in the present form, as a sensitive creative writer, he had caught some of its basic tenets. Although Hardy read no existentialist thinkers except Nietzsche, his wide observation and experience of life enabled him to know the characteristic features of the philosophy of existence. In this regard, he may be considered an existentialist thinker. It is true that Hardy read only Nietzsche and was not directly influenced by existentialism as we think of it to-day. He was conscious of existentialist ethic on account of his characteristic double vision of life and attitude. However, his awareness of the basic features of existentialism is from a literary point of view, and he is not an existentialist thinker in a wider sense. Hardy is an existentialist writer like Camus, Kafka, Mailer and Dostoevsky. In this connection, he was surely influenced by Nietzsche as his admiration for him is evident from his literary notes. Hardy read him, admired his way of life and had a high opinion of him. He expresses his admiration of Nietzsche as follows; "....Nietzsche's philosophy reaffirmed with emphasis and faith the worth of life and the splendour of human destiny", and records, "Nietzsche stands for the affirmation of life."[34]

As it is already known, the distinguishing marks of existentialism are right thought, right choice, heroic action, dedication, determination and responsibility. It insists on atheism, agnosticism, realism, humanism and optimism, and includes absurdism, dread, *angst*, anxiety, nothingness and self-alienation. It is true that these marks are evident in the life and works of Hardy. Similarly, the virtues which are necessary for man's self-realization, are also clearly reflected in the poems of Hardy though written in various moods and circumstances. Nevertheless, Hardy did not formulate any philosophical system nor did he stick to any philosophical ideas, his vision of life as expressed in his literary works is similar to that of the existentialist ethic. But many invidious critics described his view of life as pessimism and 'non-conformism' which often hurt him. As a reaction, he said; "But it is called pessimism nevertheless; under which word, expressed with contemnatory emphasis, it is regarded by many as some pernicious new thing; and the subject is charitably left to decent silence, as if further comment were needless."[35] In Hardy's theory of human reality, which he calls 'evolutionary meliorism', human existence is depicted in its bareness and frankness.

Hardy who considered his poetry as 'impression of his life', has delineated man's struggle for selfhood in its various facets. The answer to the question whether Hardy agrees with the basic tenets of existentialism mainly such as atheism, disbelief in the benevolence of religion-oriented traditional way of life and man's supremacy on the earth or not, is complicated as the majority of Hardy-critics have misunderstood him. It is true that according to Hardy's vast observation and experience of life as depicted in his work, particularly in his poetry, he seems to agree with the basic tenets of existentialist ethic.

Hardy was a firm atheist. He does not believe either in the benevolence of religion or in the existence and benevolence of God. As to the first question, the benevolence of religion, he quotes the words of John Morley; "Religion, whatever destinies may be in store for it, is at least for the present hardly any longer an organic power."[36] Similarly, about God, he writes on January 29, 1890, that "I have been looking for God for 50 years and I think that if he had existed I should have discovered him."[37] Hardy's atheism is clearly seen in his poems such as 'Hap' (WP), 'The Impercipient' (WP), 'The Bedridden Peasant' (PPP) and others. For instance, the Hardyan protagonist's dislike of God is shown in 'The Bedridden Peasant' :

> MUCH wonder I — here long low-laid-
> That this dead wall should be
> Betwixt the Maker and the made,
> Between Thyself and me!" (88)

Hardy's answer to the question whether the traditional way of life is benevolent to the existence of human beings or not is two-fold. On the one hand he thinks that the existing way of man's life is defective and should be corrected by modifications and alterations according to the necessity of time and circumstance in which he exists. On the other hand, Hardy thinks that if the old way of life cannot make life fruitful according to the changing circumstances, even though man had reconciled himself to its differences, it should be changed. Accordingly, he exhorts man to create for himself a new and modest moral and social order of life.

Hardy answers in a similar spirit the question whether man is the supreme being in the universe. Like existentialist thinkers, he accepts the view that man is the supreme being in the modern world of science and commerce. Indeed, he affirms; "An object or mark raised or made by man on a scene is worth ten times any such formed by unconscious

Nature. Hence, clouds, mists, and mountains are unimportant beside the wear on a threshold or the print of a hand."[38]

But Hardy does not believe in the benevolence of modern world of science and technology, which he feels, will never make human existence endurable. This is shown in his poem 'In Tenebris' III :

"....vision could vex or that knowledge could numb," (138)

Whatever may be the impact of science on human existence, man is the supreme being in the universe. This is mainly on account of man's will-power, action and responsibility.

Hardy agrees with the view of existentialist thinkers that though man is a part of his biological environment, the material world and his own self, he cannot always live in perfect harmony with them. However, man is an indivisible part of his biological environment, he cannot always live in perfect harmony with Nature. The main reason for this is, Nature lacks an adequate system of its own. Hardy views; "She is blind and not a judge of her actions, or that she is an automaton, and unable to control them."[39] On account of either Nature's neutrality or indifference, man alienates himself from her altogether. This is evident in Hardy's poem 'In a Wood';

Since, then, no grace I find
    Taught me of trees,
Turn I back to my kind,
    Worthy as these." (40)

However after separation from Nature, man tries to adjust himself with his community, he fails to succeed in attaining self-realization. This is because of either social codes and restrictions, or because of his own individual limitations which contribute to his destruction. The 'encouraging disapproval' of society hinders man's path of progressive enlightenment and as a result of which, man withdraws from society. This aspect of human conflict between an individual and society is apparent in Hardy's poem 'Wessex Heights' :

In the towns I am tracked by phantoms having weird
    detective ways —
Shadows of beings who fellowed with myself of earlier days:
They hang about at places, and they say harsh heavy things
Men with a wintry sneer, and women with tart disparagings."
(261)

Man after his alienation fiom society remains essentially alone. However, his solitude drags him into a world of futile doings where he is constantly haunted by dread, anxiety and confusion. Moreover, his 'internal conflicts' in which his feelings of loneliness and nothingness frustrate his designs, tear him to pieces until he is made a 'split-personality' (self-alienation). About the condition of man's self-alienation, Lakshmi Saxena says; "Such a one is enclosed within his private shell and fails to get any fresh air from the outside world."[40] This kind of man's bereaved existence is portrayed in Hardy's poem 'The Two Men' (WP).

It is in this state of inherent dread and loneliness, a self-alienated man realizes his wrong commitments. He involves himself in 'self-communion'. As a result, he realizes the importance of his biological and social environments. Similarly, he decides to be reconciled with Nature and Society, but in a different way-a way in which he retains his independence and succeeds in attaining happiness and fulfilment. In Kierkegaard's words; "By a second movement the person makes a return to the level of particularity and lives in an absolute relation to the absolute."[41] Now, his life becomes happier, enlightened and endurable. This state of an individual's self-purification and self-realization is through his healthy and harmonious reconciliation both with Nature and Society. This aspect of human life is reflected in Hardy's poems 'Great Things' and 'Conjecture'. The first poem evidences the fact that 'Man-Nature' relationship leads to man and Society's harmonious co-existence :

> O Cyder is a great thing,
> A great thing to me !
>
> . . . .
>
> O dancing is a great thing,
> A great thing to me !
>
> . . . .
>
> O love is, yes, a great thing,
> A great thing to me ! (414)

While, the second poem 'Conjecture' justifies the fact that man is a social being. In other words, man cannot live happily without the sunny atmosphere of his neighbours :

> If there were in my kalendar
> No Emma, Florence, Mary,
> What would be my existence now —

He thinks :
O were it else than this,
I'd pass to pulseless sleep ! (418)

Just as Hardy shares many ideas of existentialism, he differs also in respect of some. It is true that he agrees that there is no God, but he thinks that there is an unknown power in the universe which always hinders man's path of progress. He calls this power by various names such as 'Fate', 'Destiny', 'Crass Casualty', 'Immanent Will', and so on. According to Hardy's firm belief, this power, whatever it may be, is an incomprehensive force that certainly remains indifferent to the existence of human beings.

Hardy, like G.B. Shaw, was an 'evolutionary meliorist' who strongly believed in the gradual evolution of human existence. His 'meliorism', which includes his new faith is evident in his poetry which is truly his interpretation of life in the light of atheism and humanism. In his poetry, Hardy tries for the redemption of human existence which has become 'a world of futile doings' on account of man's inhumanity to man, woman and lower creatures.

Hardy, basically a staunch humanist, is deeply concerned with human existence in relation to man's biological environment, social world and self-consciousness. He also deals with human existence in relation to the governance of the 'world', the 'universe', and the 'Immanent Will'. He sees the world as patterned but with no meaning in it which is to be made worthwhile by man, the master of the universe. Supporting Hardy's concern for fellow-beings, Earnest Brenecke Jr. says that Hardy's sympathy for man ".... was always that of the fellow worker and fellow sufferer."[42] Hardy thought his aim was to touch the readers' heart but not to boast of his knowledge. His subject was human existence as he clearly stated in his preface to *The Poems of the Past and the Present* : ".... The road to a true philosophy of life seems to lie in humbly recording diverse readings of its phenomena as they are forced upon us by chance and change."[43] Hardy thought his duty was "...to show the sorriness underlying the grandest things, and the grandeur underlying the sorriest things." He also adds; "To find beauty in ugliness is the province of the poet."[44] Hardy's humanism is affirmed by F.B. Pinion;" His subject was 'life' and not its 'garniture' .... yet he took no interest in manners, but in the substance of life only."[45] Indeed Hardy can be summed up in the words of H.C. Duffin; "If Hardy's poetic soul had no greatness, it had beauty, tenderness, pity qualities almost as rare, and perhaps equally acceptable in the sight of the gods."[46]

People regarded him a pessimist, but in reality, Hardy is not a pessimist. He is a humanist, optimist and an evolutionary meliorist. For instance, in his 'double-vision' of life as pictured in his poetry, his protagonists are not life-deniers, they are simply rebels against the traditional way of life, superstition, religion and the dying Godhead. They do not wish to die even in the face of glaring misfortunes. They attempt to adjust with the existing situations; they reconcile their differences; and they try their best to create a new order of life which will make their life harmonious and endurable. As a result, they lead a simple, but noble and heroic life in order to achieve 'self-realization'.

REFERENCES

1. Miguel de Unamuno, qt. by John Macquarrie, *Existentialism* p. 15.
2. Karl Jaspers, *Man in the Modern Age*, tr. by Eden and Cidar Paul, p. 159.
3. J.P. Sartre, *Existentialism*, tr. by Bernard Frechtman, p. 12.
4. Karl Jaspers, 'Nature and Ethics,' *Science, Faith and Man-European Thought Since 1914*, ed. by Warren Wagner, p. 126.
5. Albert Camus, *The Rebel*, tr. by Anthony Bower, p. 263.
6. Martin Heidegger, qt. by Jean Wahl, *Philosophies of Existence*, tr. by F.M. Lory, p. 18.
7. Mary Warnock, *The Philosophy of Sartre*, p. 96.
8. J.P. Sartre, *Nausea*, tr. by L. Alexander, p. 171.
9. Merleau-Ponty, qt. by R.C. Solomon, *From Rationalism to Existentialism*, p. 307.
10. Karl Jaspers, qt. by H.J. Blackham, *Six Existentialist Thinkers*, p. 58.
11. Margaret Chatterjee, *The Existentialist Outlook*, p. 69.
12. Soren Kierkegaard, qt. by H.J. Blackham, *Six Existentialist Thinkers*, p. 11.
13. J.P. Sartre, *Existentalism*, tr. by Bernard Frechtman, pp. 44-45.
14. Thomas Hardy, 'Literary Notes', ed. by L.A. Bjork, *The Literary Notebooks of Thomas Hardy*, Vol. I, p. 366.
15. J.P. Sartre. qt. by H.J. Blackham, *Six Existentialist Thinkers*, p. 147.
16. J.P. Sartre, qt. by Emmanuel Mounier, *Existentialist Philosophies*, p. 74.
17. Soren Kierkegaard, qt. by Frederick Copleston, S.J. *A History of Modern Philosophy*, Vol. VII, part-II, p. 111.
18. Martin Heidegger, *Being and Time*, tr. by John Macqiarrie and Edward Robinson, p. 61.
19. Friedrich Nietzsche, qt. by R.C. Solomon, *From Rationalism to Existentialism*, p. 121.
20. R.A. Sinari, *Contemporary Existentialism-its limitations*, p. 13.

21. Jean Wahl, *Philosophies of Existence*, tr. by F.M. Lory, p. 31.
22. *Later Years*, p. 78.
23. Albert Camus, qt. by Margaret Chatterjee, *The Existentialist Outlook*, p. 90.
24. J.P. Sartre, *Existentialism*, pp. 37-38.
25. Karl Jaspers, qt. by Peter Koestenbaum, *The Encyclopedia of Philosophy*, Vol. IV, p. 256.
26. Soren Kierkegaard, qt. by H.J. Blackham, *Six Existentialist Thinkers*, p. 25.
27. G. Srinivasan, *Philosophical Perspectives : East and West*, p. 173.
28. Nietzsche, *The Portable Nietzsche* tr. by Walter Kaufman, p. 500.
29. Ponge qt. by E. Mounier, *Existentialist Philosophies*, p. 99.
30. Nietzsche, qt. by H. Mann *The Living Thoughts of Nietzsche*, p. 5.
31. Babur qt. by L.P. Sharma *History of Medieval India*, p. 279.
32. H. Ibsen, *An Enemy of the People*, p. 247.
33. Kierkegaard, *Kierkegaard's Anthology*, p. 429.
34. Thomas Hardy, *Literary Notes II*, Vol. II, pp. 450-451.
35. Thomas Hardy, Apology to *Late Lyrics and Earlier*, p. 557.
36. John Morley, qt. by Thomas Hardy *Literary Notes II*, Vol. II, p. 23.
37. Thomas Hardy, qt. by James G. Southworth, *The Poetry of Thomas Hardy*, p. 99.
38. *Early Life*, p. 153.
39. *Later Years*, p. 97.
40. Laxmi Saxena, *Encounter with Transcendence*, p. 18.
41. Kierkegaard, qt. by Laxmi Saxena *Encounter with Transcendence*, p. 7.
42. Ernest Brennecke Jr., *The Life of Thomas Hardy*, p. 60.
43. Thomas Hardy, Preface to *Poems of the Past and the Present*, p. 84.
44. Thomas Hardy, qt. by James Gibson and Trevor Johnson *Thomas Hardy Poems*, p. 30.
45. F.B. Pinion, 'The Ringing Vision' ed. by Lance St. John Butler *Thomas Hardy After Fifty Years*, p. 2.
46. H.C. Duffin, *Thomas Hardy*, p. 288.

3

Man and Nature in Hardy's Poetry

A detailed examination of *Wessex Poems and Other Verses* (1898) and subsequent volumes of Hardy's poetry reveals his exploration of man's suffering amidst Nature — a suffering mainly caused by man's own materialistic way of life. Similarly, we see Hardy, an evolutionary meliorist, trying in the light of existentialist ethic, to evolve a way of life which will make human existence endurable, if not happy.

The protagonists of Hardy's poems, encompassed by biological and social environments, search for a peaceful and productive way of life. As a matter of course, in the trials and tribulations they seek consolation and contentment amidst the things of Nature. However, their success or failure of attainment of selfhood in their surroundings largely depends upon their mode of relationship with Nature. Over this issue of man's ultimate relationship with his biological environment, many arguments have been put forth since the time of the 'Great Greeks'. But it is from the time of the French Revolution (1789) when Romantic literature appeared on the horizon with the doctrine of J.J. Rousseau's (1712-1778) 'Return to Nature', serious discussions about 'Man-Nature' relationship received full consideration both in literature and philosophy.

In existential philosophy, man's relationship with his biological environment has been fully expounded. On this issue, the existentialists are divided into two groups — one comprising of Heidegger, Jaspers, Ponty and Camus, and the other of Nietzsche, Kierkegaard and Sartre.

According to the first group of thinkers, Nature is stated to be attractive, loving, inspiring, kindly, friendly, glorious, sublime and magnanimous in its stature and grandeur. Jaspers, the leader of the first group, thinks that Nature is basically made to support all forms of life on earth. According to him, this is shown by her eternal cycle of production, reproduction and magnanimous presence. She is a renewable source of man's livelihood, shelter, contentment, health and happiness. She is also the promoter of harmonious human existence as well as destroyer of ugly aspects of life. Since time immemorial, it is Nature which has promoted many generations of life as well as tolerated man's ruthless atrocities. Against this background of Nature, Jaspers states that man must treat her as a being with love, faith, respect and regard. He must also know the sorrows of Nature and witness the death of her flora and fauna without any superstitious veneration or malignant enmity. Man must have special love and regard for Nature which supports all aspects of life. If she is loved and venerated man will certainly get fulfilment in her company.

On the other hand, the other group of thinkers led by Sartre rejects Jaspers' view of Nature that Nature is friendly, loving, compassionate, sublime and magnanimous. They argue that Nature is cruel, harmful, malignant and gratuitous. They say Nature can never be inspiring and compassionate to the enrichment of human existence. Sartre holds the view that Nature is neither benevolent nor neutral but it is malevolent to the existence of human beings. According to him, it is a "great gnarled paw".[1] In fact, he says, whatever Nature may be created for, it is not for the benevolence of human beings as it is a senseless destroyer and a meaningless excess.

However, these views of Jaspers and Sartre have their counterpoints in the poems of Hardy. As Nature is the background to the thought and action of his protagonists, Hardy's poems highlight and evaluate Nature's presence in both its positive and negative aspects.

Hardy's earlier poems are chiefly nature poems where Nature is depicted as a companion of human beings. Hardy's love for Nature led him to the observation of Nature's workings and its impact on the existence of human beings. He provides a broad and idealistic setting of Nature as the background in his early poems. According to him, the availability and abundance of peace, tranquillity, wealth and joy in Nature turn human life happier and endurable. He says its beauty and bounty turn human life devoid of conflicts. Several of Hardy's poems celebrate this aspect of Nature's love, warmth, compassion, inspiration and wealth.

Right from Hardy's earliest poem 'Domicilium' written in 1858, we see his preoccupation with Nature's flora and fauna. His beautiful Nature poem 'Weathers' displays how man's harmonious and fruitful relationship with Nature is a blend of love, faith, mercy, affection and veneration. The poem mirrors man's intimate relationship with Nature for help and happiness. The protagonist of the poem lives as happily as Gabriel Oak of *Far from the Madding Crowd* and Diggory Venn of *The Return of the Native*. In fact, his existence is in perfect harmony with Nature :

This is the weather the cuckoo likes,
And so do I;
When showers betumble the chestnut spikes,
And nestlings fly :
And the little brown nightingale bills his best,
And they sit outside at 'The Travellers' Rest',
And maids come forth sprig — muslin drest,
And citizens dream of the south and west,
And so do I.
This is the weather the shepherd shuns,
And so do I;
When beeches drip in browns and duns,
And thresh, and play;
And hill-hid tides throb, throe on throe,
And meadow rivulets overflow,
And drops on gate-bars hang in a row,
And rooks in families homeward go,
And so do I. (512)

Another poem 'Summer Schemes' in the same collection (LLE) reveals man's fruitful co-existence with Nature which is better than his mechanical life in the Wastelandian world of urbanized towns. Even 'Domicilium' written in Wodsworthian style, is successful in showing the positive aspects of 'Man-Nature' relationship. It describes how the old cottage was encompassed by high beeches, veil of boughs, apple trees, red roses, lilacs and green fields on hills. The poem celebrates the surroundings of Wessex heath-croppers, wood-cutters and herdsmen. The forms of life delineated in it are more in harmony with Nature than the life of their modern counterparts. Similarly, harmonious existence of the older generations who relied on Nature for most of the things is vividly depicted in 'An Unkindly May'. In this pastoral poem a simple shepherd's life with his sheep, has been shown in consonance with natural milieu. The last two lines of the poem indicate the shepherd's sense of duty :

> That shepherd still stands in that white smock-frock,
> Unnoting all things save the counting his flock. (825)

These lines remind one of the last stanza of the well-known nature poem, 'Stopping by Woods on a Snowy Evening' by Robert Frost (1874-1963) :

> The woods are lovely, dark and deep,
> But I have promises to keep,
> And miles to go before I sleep,
> And miles to go before I sleep.

The shepherd, like the protagonist of Robert Frost's poem, knows that he cannot stand in the grassland enjoying the beauty of Nature, as he has to attend to his duty. Thus the poem brings home an important fact of human existence. In fact, to support his view that man and biological environment are closely related to each other, Hardy quotes Max Muller; "We with our modern ways of life are not aware how everything we think or speak or do is dependent on the sun."[2]

Hardy regards Nature as an animate being who is powerful enough to create, recreate and destroy anything. The poet soon learns that "almost every species of tree has its voice as well as its feature. At the passing of the breeze the fir trees sob and moan no less distinctly than they rock : the holly whistles as it battles with itself; the ash hisses amid its quaverings; the beech rustles while its flat boughs rise and fall."[3] Hence, man is obliged to treat Nature as a living being which will make his existence endurable. Buber, an existentialist thinks that man's existence can be successful only if he is sufficiently devoted to Nature. He expounds; ".... in the 'I-thou' relation, we have to think of even natural entities, including inanimate objects, in terms of the relation in which they take their stand."[4]

Nevertheless, Nature in Hardy's poems does not appear either a teacher or mother as in Wordsworth's poetry. It simply appears as neutral and sometimes even as indifferent to the existence of human beings. However, it is left to man whether to be friendly or hostile towards Nature to make his life fruitful. In this regard, there is no difference of opinion between Jaspers, the existentialist thinker, and Hardy, the poet.

On a closer examination of Hardy's Nature poems, one more idea strikes us and that is his distinction between 'village life' and 'city life'. In this connection, Howard Babb remarks; "At bottom Hardy's story juxtaposes two different worlds or modes of being, the natural against the civilized and it insists on the superiority of the former by identifying the natural as strong, enduring, self-contained, slow to change, sympathetic, while associating the civilized with weakness, modernity, self centredness."[5] In Hardy's poetry, the difference between the milieu of urban life and rustic life is glaring and manifold. Urban life is depicted as complex, mechanical, deceptive and considerably erratic, whereas, rustic life is shown as simple, natural, noble and considerably harmonious. But Hardy appears to contradict himself in the following statement which is found in his notes : "If in a town lodging an honest man's daughter should have an illegitimate child; or his wife should take to drinking, he is not compelled by any squire to pack up his furniture and get his living elsewhere; as is or was lately, too often, the case in the country."[6] Kierkegaard supports Hardy's view when he speaks of his hero's failure in *Thus Spoke Zarathustra* to get a response from city people for his speech, whereas, village people readily responded. He calls city people 'crowd' and village people 'volk'. On the basis of our study of Hardy's pastoral aspects, we can conclude that his depiction of landscape portrays human existence in the countryside as primarily in consonance with the natural environment. The reason for this harmonious life of the rustics is that they primarily depend on Nature for everything. They treat her as their fellow being with love and reverence. In return, Nature provides everything which the rustic people require. As seen in Hardy's village men consult trees, air, earth, sun, rain, snow, wind, dawn and darkness, when they get down to work. Life to them is comfortable only when the earth yields abundant crops.

On the other hand, life in urban areas is quite different. It is artificial, disharmonious and erratic. According to Hardy, this is largely due to the impact of industrialization. The advent of science and technology has commercialized life and deprived man of his basic attachment to Nature. This adverse impact has not only made man independent of Nature, but also of his fellow human beings. Hardy thinks there is no greater tragedy than man's overdependence on machines for everything. Therefore, he questions; "Will not the men of the future look back with wonder on the ages in which religion, philosophy, and the science of nature were supposed to be at war, instead of being, as they will be then, one system?"[7] He observes that on account of this mishap, man's harmonious co-existence with Nature has disintegrated. Several of his poems, particularly those written after his encounter with London life in 1862, show how man's life has undergone a sea-change from that of his simple ancestor. The scientific discoveries and inventions have led to man's exploitation of Nature for his selfish interests. His knowledge and mastery over Nature has intensified this process of exploitation of natural surrounding both in its animate and inanimate forms for the glorification of his materialistic way of life. The development of science and technology has increased and intensified the wide-spread process of urbanization and industrialization resulting in a kind of chaos which man finds difficult to control. As a result, man has become complex in nature and materialistic in attitude. Hardy, a keen observer of the disturbance in the natural environment, has vividly depicted man's destruction of Nature's wealth. The following poem, 'A Backward Spring' illustrates how the trees are afraid of human disturbance :

> The trees are afraid to put forth buds,
> And there is timidity in the grass; (445)

Another poem 'Logs on the Hearth' highlights man's selfish exploitation of Nature neglecting his own good :

> The fire advances along the log
> Of the tree we felled,
> Which bloomed and bore striped apples by the peck
> Till its last hour of bearing knelled.
>
> . . . .
>
> Sawn, sapless, darkening with soot. (433)

Because of industrialization, man's exploitation of Nature has resulted in the pollution of water, weather, sound, soil and all other aspects of congenial atmosphere. Hardy's poem 'Genoa and the Mediterranean' speaks of the pollution of sea. However, Hardy, the humanist, asks the sea to put up with the inhumanity of man :

> O Epic — Famed, god-haunted Central Sea,
> Heave careless of the deep wrong done to thee (65)

Man's merciless hunting of birds is portrayed in the poem, 'The Bird-Catcher's Boy' :

Larks bruise and bleed in jail,
Trying to rise;
Every caged nightingale
Soon pines and dies.' (809)

Hardy was much sensitive and sympathetic towards the animals, birds and creatures. When asked about the condition of animals on the eve of war, he thus replied; "As a preliminary, all civilized nations might at least show their humanity by covenancing that no horse should be employed in battle except for transport. Soldiers, at worst, know what they are doing, but these animals are denied even the poor possibilities of glory and reward as a compensation for their sufferings."[8] Hardy's compassion for the dumb birds and beasts is touchingly humane. In the poem, 'The Blinded Bird' which is about the suffering of a blind bird, he asks who can be more charitable and tolerant than this blind bird who sings joyously despite of man and Nature's indignity :

Who hath charity? This bird.
Who suffereth long and is kind,
Is not provoked, though blind
And alive ensepulchred?
Who hopeth, endureth all things?
Who thinketh no evil, but sings?
Who is divine? This bird. (375)

On another occasion when he was invited to the celebration of the Royal Society for the Prevention of Cruelty towards Animals in 1924, he wrote an ode called 'Compassion'. The poem is aptly subtitled 'In Celebration of the Centenary of the Royal Society for the Prevention of Cruelty to Animals'. It is a hearty response to the cries still heard in all the secret corners of the world getting no compassionate response from human hearts :

But still those innocents are thralls
To throbless hearts, near, far, that hear no calls
Of honour towards their too — dependent frail,
And from Columbia Cape to Ind we see
How helplessness breeds tyranny
In power above assail. (805)

Florence, Hardy's second wife thought that the poem served to demonstrate the poet's passionate hatred of injustice and barbarity towards the lower creatures.

If this is man's relationship with dumb creatures what about his relation with his fellow beings? Hardy asks whether man can live with his fellow beings happily. But he finds a negative answer. Man's injustice to man makes a hell of heaven. According to him, man's greed to attain maximum benefit from Nature and to lead a luxurious life which is promised by modern science has disrupted his way of life amidst Nature in a considerable way. Above all, it has deprived him of his 'spiritual attachment' with the age old tradition of rites and rituals. That is why, both Hardy and Jaspers think that man may have knowledge and mastery over Nature's wealth, but he should not misuse them. Jaspers speculates that man may obtain whatever he requires from Nature if he devotes himself to her wishes. He declares; "Nature, once she confronts us, has a two-fold character. She is material to be used, to be consumed, and to be made; she is the object of our rule. But she is also self sufficient essence out of the depth of being."[9] Therefore, man must understand and treat her as his fellow-being, a friend and a guide; and he should treat her his companion. Otherwise, "If Nature becomes nothing but material for exploitation, the will is thrown exclusively in the direction of the quantitative..... The impoverishment of man's soul is the result of his lust for quality."[10] This view of existentialist ethic has been shared by Hardy when he quotes L.N. Tolstoi (1828-1910) : "The first condition of happiness he (T) tells us, is that the link between man and Nature shall not be broken."[11] It is owing to man's utter disregard of Nature and his ruthless exploitation of her beauty and wealth she has become not only neutral but also indifferent to his misery and suffering. Nature's neutrality towards human existence is best delineated in Hardy's 'An Autumn Rain-Scene', where Nature is portrayed as a force indifferent to a party goer; to a man hurrying to fetch saving medicament; and to a herdsman, a postman and to a coastguard :

> No care if he gain a shelter or none,
> Unhired moves one,
> On whom the rain comes down
> And another knows nought of its chilling fall
> Upon him at all,
> On whom the rain comes down. (569)

On all these personages rain comes down hampering their course of life. But this does not outweigh the fact that people just get on with things despite the natural phenomenon which often troubles them.

Nature thus due to man's attitude can be either benevolent or malevolent or neutral towards human existence.

Contrary to these views of Jaspers and the earlier Hardy that Nature is benevolent, Sartre argues that Nature can never have compassion for the misery and suffering of man. Nature he says is neither an animate being nor a conscious power to alleviate human pain. According to him, it is a 'gnarled paw' and a 'mass of biological objects'. Hardy too seems to agree with Sartre after he came under the influence of Charles Darwin, T.H. Huxley, J.S. Mill and Herbert Spencer. As his observation and experience of life grew, his view of 'Man-Nature' relationship underwent change. Subsequently, his love and veneration for Nature and his faith in her diminished in proportion to the growth of his thought. This aspect is clearly reflected in his later poems.

The poems, 'The Slow Nature', 'The Bride-Night Fire' and 'The Subalterns' show Nature's neutrality towards the misfortunes of human existence. Here Nature is presented as a destroyer of man's authentic mode of life. Pain, suffering, sickness and death are shown as indivisible parts of natural phenomenon. For instance, death in 'The Slow Nature' ends, a man's life in the form of an accident and makes his wife a prey to slow decay. When Damon hears the news of her husband John's death caused by a bull in a distant land, her agony becomes intense :

> She disappeared; and the joker stood
> Depressed by his neighbour's doom,
> And amazed that a wife struck to widowhood
> Thought first of her unkempt room.
> But a fortnight thence she could take no food,
> And she pined in a slow decay; (46)

In the long ballad 'Bride-Night Fire' another sort of tragic death by Nature's calamity is depicted. Here death lays its icy hands on a young man Tranter Sweetly when he is celebrating his wedding. It leaves his betrothed in perpetual agony. At the end of the ballad, we see how the one-day bride's life ends in frustration and failure :

> ....She said, 'I declare
> I stand as a maiden to-day!' (48)

The ballad is written in terse language, but its thought is superb as Hardy's philosophical attitude towards Nature is advanced. Likewise, in 'The Subalterns', Nature is shown an agent heaping cruelty on human beings. Here death, sickness, Nature and sky all collaborate to bring destruction to mankind :

> 'Come hither, Son,' I heard Death say;
> 'I did not will a grave
> Should end thy pilgrimage to-day,
> But I, too, am a slave!' (84)

The important notes of Hardy's thought are struck here — the suffering and helplessness of man, the inevitability of fate and the carelessness of the deities. Samuel Chew comments significantly that; "....the leaden sky, the north wind, disease, death and destruction, disclaim responsibility for the functions which they are compelled to do."[12]

In this context, one thing must be borne in mind that Nature is not only cruel to human beings but also to birds, beasts and trees. Nature's indifference to them is shown in 'The Bullfinches' :

> All we creatures, nigh and far
> (Said they there), the Mother's are;
> Yet she never shows endeavour
> To protect from warrings wild
> Bird or beast she calls her child. (86)

This sort of sorrow and disappointment of 'birds' and 'beasts' has resulted because of Nature's want of sufficient food and fodder for its creatures. The same theme is reflected in another poem, 'Winter in Durnover Field' where birds find no grain and as a result starve :

> *Starling* : "Aye : patient pecking now is vain
> Throughout the field, I find ....
> *Rook* : No Grain! (117)

Here the repetition of the phrases 'no grain throughout the land' and 'encrusted with frost' indicates Nature's full indifference to the existence of birds. As the seasons worsen birds and beasts migrate in search of food, or starve. On the other hand, are the species in Nature free from conflicts ? Hardy's 'In a Wood' which is about Nature's indifference towards man, gives a negative answer :

> Even the rank poplars bear
> Lothly a rival's air,
> Cankering in black despair
> If overborne. (40)

Similarly, the condition of peasants is not enduring due to natural calamities like floods and droughts. Moreover, on account of social conflicts, political oppression and psychological tensions, the life of agriculturists in rural areas has been degenerated. As a whole, man's co-existence with Nature is not fruitful. Consequently, everything is in disorder and disintegration. As a keen observer Hardy puts it thus; " 'The labourers have become more and more migratory', and as a consequence village tradition, a vast mass of unwritten folklore, local chronicle, local topography, and nomenclature — is absolutely sinking, has nearly sunk, into eternal oblivion."[13] In a majority of Hardy's poems, Nature appears malevolent. It looks an impediment to the course of human progress and enlightenment :

> So savage winter catches
> The breath of limber things,
> And what I love he snatches,
> And what I love not, brings. (162)

When Hardy came under the influence of Charles Darwin, J.S. Mill, T.H. Huxley, Herbert Spencer, Sir Charles Lyell, Sir Leslie Stephen and a host of other leading biologists, thinkers and philosophers, his view of man's ultimate relationship with Nature underwent a change. In the new perspective, he feels that 'Man-Nature' relationship usually ends in aberration. Accordingly, he made an entry in his diary in 1887 : "I feel that Nature is played out as a Beauty, but not a Mystery. I don't want to see landscapes, i.e., scenic paintings of them, because I don't want to see the original realities — as optical effects, that is, I want to see the deeper reality underlying the scenic, the expression of what are sometimes called abstract imagination."[14] As a result, he begs her :

> Show thee as I thought thee
> When I early sought thee. (37)

Hardy questions Nature whether she alleviates the suffering of human beings caused by her :

> When wilt thou wake, O Mother, wake and see —
> . . . .
> The coils that thou hast wrought unwittingly;
> . . . .
> Wilt thou destroy, in one wild shock of shame,
> Thy whole high heaving firmamental frame,
> Or patiently adjust, amend, and heal? (85)

The poet regrets that Nature neither adjusts nor amends her infliction of misery on man unwittingly wrought by her calamities. He regrets that instead of consoling the suffering human beings, Nature remains neutral. The poem 'Last Look round St. Martin's Fair' displays the outright malevolence of not only Nature but also of the whole universe to mankind :

The sun is like an open furnace door,
Whose round revealed retort confines the roar
  Of fires beyond terrene;
The moon presents the lustre-lacking face
  Of a brass dial gone green,
Whose hours no eye can trace.
The unsold heathcroppers are driven home. (730)

Hardy's later view of Nature is explained by David Cecil and J.R. Brooks. The former remarks; "....he (Hardy) would have been disinclined to worship it even if it had possessed a soul, for nature, to Hardy, was far from being all beauty and goodness. It had its beautiful aspects and no one appreciated them more sensitively but it had other aspects too : cruelty, indifference and caprice. Indeed, in nature he saw repeated the same blind and selfish struggle that he found in the life of man."[15] In fact, she is engaged in constant destruction and devising ways and means of torturing them with impunity. J.R. Brooks thinks that Hardy sounds the death knell of the old romantic views of nature poetry. But, Nature is not affected by the suffering of human beings. Like a hard-hearted criminal, she is sitting on her throne with the gesture of an immovable dictator whose word is unchangeable malignant law.

However, like Gautam Buddha, Hardy thinks that ignorance is the main cause of human misfortunes. He is of the view that pain and suffering are essential accompaniments of human life. They are so powerful as to swallow joy and happiness which sometimes suffuse life and put people into the illusory world of happiness and contentment. He thinks that happiness is an illusion and punished are those who seek it. Because happiness is a temporary cessation of desire. Desire is an expression of a want. It is, in fact, a form of pain. Therefore, happiness is the deliverance from pain and it is only a negative, and never a positive state. When Nature is viewed and explored only for man's materialistic purposes, when she is ruthlessly exploited and treated as an instrument, man can never get peace, tranquillity and spiritual consolation from her. It is true, owing to man's exploitation of Nature's resources, there is every possibility of impoverishment of human soul and an utter degradation of human values. Therefore, Nietzsche considering science as the root cause of degeneration of human life describes it as " '...transformation of Nature into concepts for the purpose of governing Nature'."[16] The advanced knowledge and the progress of civilization do not improve matters as science simply brings with it problems which can never be solved in the present situation. Similarly, the so-called virtues, whatever they may be, which float in the air of the modern world of science are merely refined egoism. The chief limitation of science is its incompleteness, and on account of man's materialism, there is no escape for man from the pangs of suffering in Nature. Subsequently, life like a pendulum, oscillates between joy and sorrow. Therefore, Arthur Schopenhauer aptly remarks, "In much wisdom is much grief; and he that increaseth knowledge increaseth sorrow."[17] Hardy writes to a friend; " 'What we gain by science is, after all, sadness....the more we know of the laws and nature of the universe, the more ghastly a business one perceives it all to be', and it is among the uneducated, that happiness will find her last refuge on earth, since it is among them that a perfect insight into the conditions of existence will be longest postponed".[18] Confirming Hardy's view, J.I.M. Stewart thinks that human life is everywhere a state in which much is to be endured and little to be enjoyed. Nature can be trusted enough but Hardy adds that the degrading materialism gives man more pain than pleasure. According to him, the Prime Mover whether personified as either 'love' or 'chance' or 'Nature' persuades us to a world which is devoid of virtues that support human existence. In T.S. Eliot's (1888-1968) words such a world is aptly called Pure Evil or Westeland. Therefore, Hardy remarks, ".... to model our conduct on Nature's apparent conduct, ...can only bring disaster to humanity".[19] Even existentialists think that the indifference of Nature falsifies our calculations and betrays our hopes. Accordingly if man lives amidst Nature with a hope of self realization, he will become a victim of circumstance. Upholding this, Tom Paulin says that to Hardy, Nature seemed a ruined church. Whatever Nature offers to man, behind it lies the greater indifference to the lot of him. Moreover, 'natural laws' hamper the course of human life. Thus, Nature's state of unconsciousness leads creatures to mourn and decay as we have seen in the foregoing extracts.

Hardy, like other existentialist thinkers, comes to the conclusion that man's place both in Nature and universe is comparatively insignificant. He thinks on account of his mortality and finitude in the eternity of time and space man's role is unworthy. This is vividly reflected in 'An August Midnight' and 'Yall'ham Wood's Story'. For instance, the first poem reflects the view that man's place in the universe is of little importance :

> Thus meet we five, in this still place,
> At this point of time, at this point in space. (113)

Hardy goes further to say that man's life is not merely a tragedy, but Life makes deliberately and vindictively more tragic by first giving him a hope but denying it later. In fact, hopes are seen to be dupes. This may be seen in 'Yell'ham-Wood's Story' :

> Coomb – Firtrees say that Life is a moan,
> And Clyffe-hill Clump says 'Yea!'
> But Yell'ham says a thing of its own :
> . . . .
> It says that Life would signify
> A thwarted purposing :
>
> That we come to live, and are called to die.
> Yes, that's the thing
> In fall, in spring,
> That Yell'ham says :
> 'Life offers — to deny!' (244)

Hardy thinks that the universe in which man struggles is infinite in time and space. It is true that man is a powerless entity in Nature, Society and Universe, and the tragic force that rules his destiny certainly overrides his will.

Hardy's mental depression about man's insignificance in universe can be traced to the influence of Arthur Schopenhauer's *The World As Will and Idea* (1881), J.S. Mill's *On Nature* (1858) and *On Liberty* (1859), Charles Darwin's *Origin of the Species* (1859) and *Descent of Man* (1863), Von Hartmann's *The Philosophy of the Unconsciousness* (1869) and the works of Sir Charles Lyell, William Herschel and others. Charles Darwin proved that man and monkey were collateral descendents of a single ancestor and the earth where man struggles is much older than his ancestors. Furthermore, modern science and technology brought the traditional way of life to an end and made human life extremely complex.

However, man's insignificance both in Nature and Universe does not diminish and destroy his conscience, fortune, power and glory. It will never weaken his 'will-power' which is stronger than the Nature and Universe. Hence, man who is an emotional, rational, social and intellectual being, may certainly assert his personal choice and achieve perfection.

To sum up the foregoing views and observations of 'Man-Nature' relationship in Hardy's poetry, we come to the conclusion that 'Man-Nature' relationship is fruitful so long as man has love, veneration and regard for her. If he harbours ill-will towards her or she remains indifferent to his mode of existence, he alienates himself from her and seeks consolation and contentment amidst his fellow human beings :

> Since, then, no grace I find
> Taught me of trees,
> Turn I back to my kind,
> Worthy as these. (40)

Whatever may be the reason for man's inevitable alienation from Nature, both Hardy and existentialists boldly assert that man's active detachment from his biological surrounding will not weaken him. According to them, his separation from Nature will be counterbalanced by his superiority of conscience and heroic action. They think that man through his heroic mode of life, may alleviate the pain and suffering caused by natural phenomena. Hardy says man through his peaceful and productive way of life with his fellow beings may attain self-realization. In existentialism as well as in Hardy's poetry, the superiority of man's consciousness, will-power, action and responsibility for self-realization has been upheld and glorified. Both existentialist thinkers and Hardy uphold the view that man is the master of all things. In this regard Hardy concludes; "An object or mark raised or made by man on a scene is worth ten times any such formed by Unconscious Nature. Hence clouds, mists, and mountains are unimportant beside the wear on a threshold, or the print of a hand."[20] In this way he claims man's inherent freedom and responsibility for his ultimate self-realization.

REFERENCES

1. J.P. Sartre, qt. by Marry Warnock, *The Philosophy of Sartre*, p. 94.
2. Thomas Hardy, *Literary Notes I*, Vol. I, p. 168.

3. Thomas Hardy, qt. by Carl J. Weber, *Hardy of Wessex*, p. 10.
4. Martin Buber, 'The Elusive Mind and the I-Thou' ed. by H.D. Lewis, *The Elusive Mind*, p. 246.
5. Howarb Babb, qt. by Ian Gregor, *The Great Web : The Form of Hardy's Fiction*, p. 50.
6. *Life*, p. 46.
7. Thomas Hardy, *Literary Notes I*, Vol. I, p. 66.
8. *Later Years*, p. 81.
9. Karl Jaspers, 'Existential Ethics', edited by Warren Wagner, *Science, Faith and Man-European Thought Since 1914*, p. 130.
10. *Ibid.*, p. 131.
11. Thomas Hardy, *Literary Note II*, Vol. II, p. 16.
12. Samuel Chew, *Thomas Hardy : Poet and Novelist*, p. 176.
13. *Life*, p. 46.
14. *Life*, p. 31.
15. David Cecil, *Hardy The Novelist : An Essay in Criticism*, p. 67.
16. Friedrich Nietzche, qt. by Frederick Copleston S.J., *A History of Philosophy*, Vol. 7, p. 183.
17. Arthur Schopenhauer, qt. by Frank Thilley, *History of Philosophy*, p. 500.
18. Thomas Hardy, qt. by J.I. M. Stewert, *Thomas Hardy : A Critical Biography*, p. 35.
19. *Ibid.*, p. 42.
20. *Early Life*, p. 153.

4

Man and Society in Hardy's Poetry

'We wonder, ever wonder, why we find us here!'

When Nature becomes a destroyer of harmonious human existence, preventing human beings from attaining perfection, man turns to his fellow-beings for harmonious co-existence through which he hopes to attain selfhood. As a result, his attachment to his community becomes inevitable. In Hardy's presentation of human beings and their mode of life, we clearly observe his protagonists' struggle to adjust with others after their inevitable psychic detachment from their biological environment. Many critics wonder as to why many of Hardy's protagonists do not adjust with Nature. The reasons for the failure of 'Man-Nature' relationship in Hardy's poems are varied. However, there are mainly two reasons which unfailingly spoil 'Man-Nature' relationship. Firstly man himself is hostile to Nature on account of his materialistic attitude and his desire for controlling the biological sphere. So, he has begun to live at the cost of natural phenomena. In fact, he has become ambitious to lead a luxurious life which is promised by modern science. In turn, this has resulted in the second reason — Nature's consequent indifference towards human existence. Owing to man's injudicious exploitation of Nature's beauty and bounty, a kind of natural imbalance is created. Subsequently, this has led to natural calamities disrupting human lives in a considerable way. Therefore, Hardy says; "....to model our conduct on Nature's apparent conduct, ... can only bring disaster to humanity."[1] Thus, man feels that Nature is not only neutral but also indifferent to his wishes. Therefore, he cannot help withdrawing himself from Nature in order to lead a happy life amidst his fellow beings. These two reasons have characterized 'Man-Nature' relationship as 'I-It' rather than 'I-Thou'. Accordingly, man who realizes that he cannot lead a fruitful life amidst Nature, alienates himself from her. This is vividly shown in Hardy's nature poem 'In a Wood' where the protagonist resolves to live amidst his own folk as the things in Nature appear to be at discord :

Even the rank poplars bear
Lothly a rival's air,
Cankering in black despair
If overborne.

. . . .

There at least smiles abound,
There discourse trills around,
There, now and then, are found
Life-loyalties. (40)

The poem, thematically opposed to Wordsworth's 'Tables Turned', displays the clash between Nature's different species which ultimately lead to rivalry and destruction. This convinces man of his need to reconcile himself to his fellow-beings for 'life-loyalties'.

Man's alienation from his biological environment compels him to have personal and social relationship. As a result, an individual tries to have sexual and social relationships with 'Other' and 'Others' respectively. Here, the 'Other' stands for one's partner and the 'Others' for the community. In the philosophy of existence, an individual's personal relationship with his spouse is built more on biological factors than on economical and sociological grounds. Subsequently, the partner is not a means but an end and the relationship between man and woman is to be based on love, regard and sacrifice. Moreover, the negative emotions such as cruelty, selfishness, disregard and hostility have to be avoided. Even the discordant distinctions like class, caste and creed based either on economic factors or dogmatic beliefs should be undermined. Similarly, there should not be sexual incompatibility between man and woman. In existentialism this mode of 'Man-Woman' relationship is characterized by 'I-Thou'. On the whole 'Man-Woman' relationship has to be ideal if man and woman are to attain selfhood.

Wessex poems delineate 'Man-Woman' relationship on a broader scale and in a variety of social settings. While dealing with 'Man-Woman' relationship, Hardy thinks that there must be equivalence, openness, confidence, willingness and mutual understanding between man and woman for harmonious co-existence. There must not be egoism, indifference, disbelief, disunity and sexual incompatibility between sexual partners as these vices cause serious psychological tensions and widen the rift between them. But Hardy gives more freedom to woman, partly because of her necessity to bring up children, and partly because of her weakness and gentleness. He values the indispensable role of woman in man's life. According to him; "Without women, the beginning of our life would be helpless; the middle, devoid of pleasure; and the end, of consolation."[2] Even in existentialism, philosophers like Jaspers and Sartre give priority to womanhood for the betterment of familial life.

Man and woman's harmonious life characterized by love, faith, respect and regard is depicted in Hardy's poem 'The Dance at the Phoenix'. Here a woman named Jenny is quite happy with her husband as 'love' becomes a means of transcendental bliss to her :

> She kissed him long, as when, just wooed,
> She chose his domicile.
> She felt she would give more than life
> To be the single-hearted wife. (28)

Their cordial relationship is a key that opens the door to their fulfilment and selfhood. In this connection, Hardy stresses one more virtue, that is, love blended with mercy and sacrifice for a closer relationship between man and woman.

But the majority of Hardy's poems are about the failed human relationship on account of either man or woman's lack of congenial virtues like love, fidelity, self-sacrifice, endearment, adjustment and willingness to co-operate with the spouse. Many of the leading thinkers of the ages have hotly debated over the issue of the failure of 'Man-Woman' relationships. But none of them has given adequate justification and solution to this eternal problem. Nevertheless, some thinkers have tried to trace the causes of broken relationships or an individual's alienation from others. Existentialist thinkers believe that the reason for this crisis is man's superiority complex, desire to dominate others and to amass wealth for personal glcry. They opine that the society as a collective entity becomes responsible for an individual's ruin. It is true, since the dawn of human history, all civilized societies have been dominant on account of the doctrine 'might is right' (Social Darwinism). Subsequently these vices *i.e.*, 'male dominance', 'greed for possession' and 'indifference of society' have created an everlasting confusion and conflict in human life.

Corresponding to the levels on which human beings exist, three reasons may be noted for man's alienation from his fellow-beings :

(1) Psychological reason corresponding to the psychological level.

(2) Social reason corresponding to the social level.

(3) Sexual reason corresponding to the instinctual level.

On the psychological level, cynicism, erratic behaviour, maladjustment and misunderstanding of either man or woman, can often hinder the course of their life. Eventually this leads to conflicts and clashes between the two, and it would result in the defeat of both. Hardy attributes this misfortune to man's inflexible nature. Therefore he states; "We can't change the essence of our being....(by education)....but we can ....make our faults useful", and according to him, "To do this is the great problem and secret of education".[3] In similar spirit, Buber thinks that man can never change the nature of others according to his desire. This is an eternal problem. This sort of psychic failure between man and woman is reflected in Hardy's sonnet series 'She, to Him'. In these sonnets which depict the failure of 'Man-Woman's relationship, a gentle woman submits herself to her husband, but the hard-hearted man does not respond to her desires. The scene is genuine :

> I will be faithful to thee; aye, I will! (16)

But he says;

> This love puts all humanity from me;
> I can but maledict her, pray her dead, (17)

Similarly, the poem 'A Broken Appointment' reveals misunderstanding as the chief factor for the failure of 'Man-Woman' relationships :

> You did not come,
> And marching Time drew on, and wore me numb.-
> . . . .
> Grieved I, when, as the hope-hour stroked its sum,
> You did not come.
>
> You love not me,
> And love alone can lend you loyalty;
> . . . .
> You love not me? (99)

The repetition of the lines 'You did not come' and 'You love not me' emphasizes the lover's disappointment, loneliness and grief in the absence of his beloved. The poem is vivid and moving but bitter in tone.

Secondly, social distinctions, such as class (Europe), creed (Africa) and caste (Asia) mar peace and harmony in 'Man-Woman' relationships. The rigid structure of social systems deprive man and woman what they truly deserve. As a result, the partners are estranged from each other leading to mutual ruin. This is reflected in many of Hardy's poems. It is due to the erratic marriage system that Tess suffers in the poem 'Tess's Lament' (PPP) and in Hardy's novel *Tess of the D'Urbervilles*. It is her confession that lands her into trouble just as it does in the novel of that name. In this connection, Hardy thinks 'male dominance' and the 'rigidities of marriage system' lead the innocent to debasement and unwilling submission. That is why in his preface to *Jude the Obscure* he writers; ".... a marriage should be dissolvable as soon as it becomes a cruelty to either of the parties."[4] The poems 'A Poor Man and a Lady' (HS) and 'The Revisitation' (TL) display how the rich ladies reject poor men when they propose marriage. In the first poem, a poor man asks a rich lady to marry him in vain :

> We could do no better; and thus it stood
> Through a time of timorous secret bliss,
> Till we were divided, and never a kiss
> Of mine could touch you, or likelihood. (766)

This story about an aristocratic lady's indifference towards a poor man was the theme of Hardy's first novel *A Poor Man and a Lady* (1867) which was never published and was later turned into a long short story. The theme of broken 'Man-Woman' relationship with a little variation is echoed in 'The Orphaned Old Maid' and 'Her Father' (TL). In the first poem an ill-willed father prevents his daughter from marrying so that she will look after him in his old age. But, after his death, it is too late for her to marry. Hardy has delineated her tragic tale with great clarity and ingenuity. The poems 'Cross-Currents' (LLE), 'The Difference' (SC) and 'The Division' (TL) demonstrate the fact that married life can hardly run smooth. These poems show that married partners fall apart on account of disunity caused by the trials and tribulations of life. In these poems, partners lack genuine virtues. Hence their life is disintegrated and their joy and progress are spoiled. Hardy's critical assessment of the marriage system, divorce and other social rigidities takes a philosophical colouring in poems like 'A Poor Man and a Lady' (HS) and 'A Question of Marriage' (WW). It is true that on account of his bitter experience in married life which is explicit in "Poems of 1912-13" subtitled *Veteris Vestigia flammae* in *Satires of Circumstance, Lyrics and Reveries*, Hardy came to the conclusion that social distinctions and disparities hardly enable human beings to lead a fruitful married life.

A close inspection of Hardy's poems reveals that 'Man-Woman' relationship can also suffer on account of sexual incompatibility. Hardy admits that because of sexual incompatibility man and woman may fail to come close together even though they are on the same social and intellectual level. This is clear in his poems 'Lost Love' (SC) and 'The Burghers' (WP). These poems show different aspects of 'Man-Woman' broken relationships merely on the ground of sexual factors. For instance, in the "Lost Love" a woman feels frustrated, for her husband has failed to satisfy her earthly desires :

> So I wait for another morn,
> And another night
> In this soul-sick blight;
> And I wonder much
> As I sit, why such
> A woman as I was born ! (259)

The theme of sexual incompatibility and its evil consequence are best revealed in 'The Burghers'. Here a woman's desire for illicit love and her consequent elopement puzzles her husband. However, the understanding husband lets her go with her lover. He also allows her to take her belongings; and bids them adieu as if his head and heart were cold :

> With eye and cry of love illimited
> Upon her Heart-king. Never upon me
> . . . .
> 'I'll take you to the doorway in the wall,
> And then adieu,' I told them. 'Friends, withdraw'.
> They did so; and she went-beyond recall. (23)

The scene recalls the situation of the estrangement between Richard Phillotson and his wife Sue Bridehead in Hardy's last novel *Jude the Obscure*. In these poems, Hardy thinks that married life often undergoes strange vicissitudes due to sexual incompatibility. The theme affords Hardy an admirable opportunity to display his dramatic power.

In addition to sexual incompatibility, the evils of marriage system further complicate and worsen the matter. In fact, social rigidities hardly allow man to reconcile his differences. But Hardy offers a solution to this crisis. According to him, youths who are eager to marry must think whether they will succeed in their married life before they enter the marriage bond. He advises them to understand their respective partners and try to adjust themselves with them. He thinks married people must have knowledge of sexual problems and must be capable of solving them. Even the existentialist thinkers Sartre and Jaspers are of the same view when they emphasize on the virtues of love, fidelity, equality, respect, regard and mutual understanding between the married partners. Hardy attributes the failure of 'Man-Woman' relationship to haste and misunderstanding. He writes; "... marry in haste and repent at leisure".[5] Indeed, many of his poems are on the theme of estranged and failed relationships. According to critics, many of his poems have themes of disastrous or betrayed or merely boring sexual relationships. J.I.M. Stewart aptly observes; "Alike in love and marriage, the characters of Hardy's poems are perpetually getting themselves into luckless situations.[6]

In this way, 'Man-Woman' relationships on the grounds of psychological, social and sexual factors fail and culminate either in estrangement or in mutual ruin. Hardy says this is because of man's egoism, enmity and rigid taste and temperament. He remarks; "As to error, we are always changing it, but we never get rid of it ...."[7] Thus, it is due to man's inherent weakness and limitations, 'Man-Woman' relationship fails. Nevertheless love once thought to be a means of man's harmonious life, has ceased to be so. This is attributed either to man or woman's greed for 'possession' and 'domination'. As life is measured according to its practical values, all life-generating values are either ignored or misused on the pretext of material advancement. This is revealed by the study of the conflict of the sexes in Hardy's poems written in different social settings.

According to Hardy, love cannot lead to 'life-loyalties' in a society which is based on rigidities. Indeed, in his poem 'I Said to Love', the protagonist speculates that love in the bygone days was 'one which spread a heaven beneath the sun'. But the modern way of life which is largely materialistic, has turned the good old way of life into suffering. Therefore, in Hardy's poem love is asked to depart from human heart :

'Depart then, Love ! ....
— Man's race shall perish, threatenest thou,
Without thy kindling coupling-vow?
The age to come the man of now
Know nothing of ?-
We fear not such a threat from thee;
We are too old in apathy!
Mankind shall cease. — So let it be,'
I said to Love. (77)

A deserted lover in the poem 'Revulsion' (WP), affirms that his 'heart's table bear no woman's name'. Likewise, a lover in 'Song to Aurore' (WW) thinks that 'Life is a labour' and 'Kisses are caresome things!'. Therefore, in his gloomy mood, the poet thinks that the power of love neither leads to psychological ascendancy nor to the attainment of selfhood.

Just the same man's relationship with society is found to be on decline. Hardy as well as existentialist thinkers opines that 'Man-Society' relationship will succeed if the virtues like love, faith, friendship, sacrifice, broad mindedness, mutual understanding, respect and regard are adopted. This mode of social relationship which is characterised by 'I-Thou' in existentialist terminology, brings peaceful and productive co-existence between an individual and society. In case these virtues are neglected, a happy relationship between an individual and society will be impossible. That is why an individual must try to adjust with the larger community in order to achieve his objects. If he thinks he is superior to the community he will involve himself in everlasting conflicts which, in turn, will make him an alien to his community. Therefore, Hardy says every one either in a family or in society should try to understand one another and should not try to dominate others. In this regard, he quotes a Flemmish poet Jakob Van Marlant : "Two words exist in the world, *mine* and *thine*. If they could be suppressed peace would reign and all would be free".[8]

Some of Hardy's poems celebrate harmonious social relationships. This mode of life based on humanitarian doctrines carries man very far on the path of progress. The poem 'Queen Caroline to Her Guests' displays a person's desire to have companions for a worthwhile co-existence. Here a rich lady requests her guests to remain with her for spiritual betterment :

Dear friends, stay!
Lamplit wafts of wit keep sorrow
In the limbo of to-morrow :
Dear friends, stay! (711)

As a social being man requires a good society. No doubt for this Hardy emphasises on the need of a healthy society based on individual spontaneity and prosperity-oriented values. He observes; "I consider a social system based on individual spontaneity to promise better for happiness than a curbed and uniform one under which all temperaments are bound to shape themselves to a single pattern of living. To this end I would have society divided into groups of temperaments, with a different code of observance for each group."[9] Man is a social animal. His cognitive activity is not an end in itself but is intended to sub-serve the needs of his purposive life. He is not a mere 'spectator' in the world, but an active agent who is involved with others and his cognitive observation arises only in the course of his purposive activities in life. Consequently, man's existence and attainment of essence is closely related to the social phenomenon. This involvement of man with others is fundamental for the realization of selfhood and transcendental bliss. Hardy's autobiographical poem 'Conjecture' illustrates this point :

If there were in my kalendar
No Emma, Florence, Mary,
What would be my existence now-
A hermit's ? - wanderer's weary?-
How should I live, and how
Near would be death, or far?

He thinks in their absence :

O were it else than this,
I'd pass to pulseless sleep! (418)

Hardy tender and genial at heart and jovial in personal life, thinks that society is indispensable for the enrichment of life. This view is also reflected in existentialism. Sartre who insists on individual's liberty, agrees that man's being-in-the society is basically being-with-others. Both Hardy and Sartre seem to think that man's co-existence with society is a basic phenomenon.

Nevertheless, on many occasions, man's relationship with society is not at all easy and worthwhile. This is because of the hostility of society towards a flourishing individual. Secondly, as an individual, man is also responsible for his failure to succeed in inter-personal relationships. His ambition to lead a luxurious mode of life even at the cost of others, automatically spoils his relationship with his community. The two factors, 'society's indifference' and 'individual's greed for domination' strain inter-personal relationships and bring hostility and ruin. It is true that man's relationship with his community will not be in perfect harmony. Hardy says 'Man-Society' relationship will not be harmonious so long as man and society do not agree about human values. If there is no proper understanding between an individual and community, man's inter-personal relationship is naturally bound to fail. This is revealed in 'In Tenebris' I, II and III and in 'Wessex Heights'. In the poem 'In Tenebris I', a deserted man is not happy because the society has brought disgrace upon him. As a result he has no hopes either in his family life or in community life. Hence, he cannot help waiting in 'unhope' :

> Black is night's cope;
> But death will not appall
> One who, past doubtings all,
> Waits in unhope. (136)

However, the alienated man neither loses his strength nor he is afraid of death. Of course, his heart is smitten and withered like grass. Here the images 'leaves' and 'grass' symbolize the frailty of human existence. Moreover, Nature is depicted as bleak, but that does not frighten him as he has already separated himself from it. But the horrible thing is that his fellow beings are bleaker within their own souls. The poem is a successful lyric emphasizing the futility of human life in society.

The second poem 'In Tenebris' has longer lines which highlight the greater depth of the alienated man's bereavement. His life has become a nightmare as he has been abused by society for his adventures. He is also condemned to solitude. However, the protagonist does not think that 'the world is a bad place'. He only feels that evils do exist in order to spoil harmony and progress. Though the people think that 'All's well' the victim realizes that he is a man 'born out of due time' and he has no calling in society. This happens because the latter 'exacts a full look at the Worst' and happiness, a delicate thing, is 'cramped by crookedness, custom, and fear'. So he questions himself :

> Then what is the matter is I, I say. Why should
> such an one be here?.... (137)

In the poem the 'Clash of the first' refers to the biblical legend in which Abel was killed by his brother Cain. Hardy seems to have used this allusion to reinforce the fact that man is basically cruel towards his brethren and other creatures. But Hardy does not deny the possibility of happiness through an authentic mode of existence. Supporting this, Merryn Williams affirms; "Hardy is asking that human beings should be honest about the imperfect state of the world they live in, rather than insisting that everything was for the best in the best of all possible worlds."[10] The Latin motto of 'In Tenebris' II " 'Considerabam ad dexteram, et videbam; et non erat qui cognosert me....non est qui requirat animam meam.' " means : "I looked on my right hand, and beheld, but there was no man that would know me....no man cared for my soul' ". The poem certainly highlights the indifference of society towards an individual.

Similarly in the third poem 'In Tenebris' the protagonist dislikes man's greed for knowledge which brings more pain than pleasure. He seems to think that knowledge may be true in the abstract but doubtful in its application to human situations. Therefore he desires to die rather than live in the present society which is a welter of futile doings. This is corroborated by Hardy when he states; "People are not more humane, so far as I can see, than they were in the year of my birth."[11] Hardy, a staunch humanist finds solution to this conflict through peaceful negotiation and reconciliation. His love and compassion for the isolated individual has really been much appreciated. These fine lyrical poems show man's loneliness and pain, unrelieved both by Nature and Society.

Like his contemporary poet A.E. Housman, Hardy writes about the theme of hostile social relationship with an individual, and man's eventual alienation from it. In fact, he drives home the fact that there is always a kind of conflict between an individual and society. This is seen in the poem 'Wessex Heights'. Here the belligerence of society towards a peace-loving man is at its height :

> In the lowlands I have no comrade, not even the lone
> man's friend —
> . . . .
> In the towns I am tracked by phantoms having weird
> detective ways —
> . . . .
> They hang about at places, and they say harsh heavy
> things —

> Men with a wintry sneer, and women with tart
> disparagings. (261)

These long twisted lines certainly denote the protagonist's frustration and disappointment in society. In the town he is tracked by phantoms of cynical eyes as it (society) is filled with 'men of a wintry sneer'. As a result, he alienates himself from society in search of transcendental bliss. The indifference of society to an individual who is in search of selfhood causes his alienation from it altogether. Moreover, the co-incidence of fate also hinders such man's happiness, peace and prosperity, and according to Hardy, it piles chance upon chance to take him unaware. However, such an alienated individual should not bothere of, and instead, he should be confident of getting a new mode of life in isolation. In this regard, his unhappy life in society is counter balanced by his will-power, superior consciousness, right thought and choice, heroic action and responsibility.

Existentialist thinkers uphold man's alienation from society as they think man, in order to lead a free and responsible life, should alienate himself from society which is an 'arrested mode of life'. In Jaspers view non-alienation from society throws man into frustration and abyss of nothingness. Hence, he considers alienation a "means of encounter with 'Transcendence' "[12] In a similar spirit, Sartre opines that life in society is something 'unbecoming' of the dignity of man. Likewise Heidegger regards alienation, a necessary condition for a responsible life. Here a kind of 'ethical alienation' in which the individual becomes intensely aware of his individuality and freedom is insisted upon as the most desirable condition of human life.

This view is reflected in Hardy's poem 'Wessex Heights' where the protagonist who is meditating over his past on his favorite Wessex Heights, does not wish to go to the 'great grey plain' that is nothing but 'society' :

> I cannot go to the great Plain; there's a figure
> against the moon.
> Nobody sees it but I, and it makes my breast beat out
> of tune; (261)

However, the aftermath of alienation brings a sort of dread, anxiety, anguish and nothingness. In this situation, everything seems to be in confusion. As a result, man feels despair whenever he has to take a momentous decision of immense consequence. In fact, as Heidegger observes, to such man, "The whole world seems to be slipping away from oneself in this mood of dread."[13] The aftermath of alienation that brings 'dread' and 'anguish' which are threatening is reflected in 'In Tenebris' II :

> The bolt seems straightway in me alone; one better
> he were not here. (137)

Man's alienation from society becomes indispensable on account of society's hostility towards his progress and enlightenment. Therefore Kierkegaard asks; "Is the individual supported in his quest for selfhood, by the solidarity of human society" (?).[14] In a similar spirit J.S. Mill, a renowned social reformer of England states; "Society... practises a social tyranny more formidable than many kinds of political oppression, since, though not usually upheld by such extreme penalties, it leaves fewer means of escape, penetrating much more deeply into the details of life, and enslaving the soul itself."[15] An utter indifference of society towards an individual is vividly delineated in Hardy's 'The Church-Builder'. In this poem, a theist who sacrifices everything for the glorification of God, is severely criticised by his neighbours :

> The deeper thinkers sneer and smirk,
> And give my toil no mind;
> From nod and wink
> I read they think
> That I am fool and blind." (139)

Another aspect of Hardy's poetic thought found in this regard is his dislike of 'Social Darwinism'. Though, Charles Darwin who published his monumental work. *Origin of the Species* in 1859, did not uphold the view that 'might is right', the later materialists have upheld the theory of the 'survival of the fittest'. Particularly the British glorified this theory of evolution for their materialistic justifications and benefits. Even though this was not accepted everywhere, the people of weaker sections were victimized. But Hardy criticised Social Darwinism. He also criticised the imperialistic design which England imposed in her colonies. He referred this to the "... great and eternal incongruity of man's existence — the conflict of a spiritual nature and such aspirations as man's with conditions entirely physical."[16] This is evident in his poems written on Boer, Napoleanic and the first World War. His poem 'The Man He Killed' shows modern man's cruelties perpetrated in pride of power and glory. The poem illustrates this point of view when a soldier kills his companion just because he was in the enemie's camp :

'I shot him dead because —
Because he was my foe,
Just so: my foe of course he was;
That's clear enough; although. (236)

According to Hardy man's desire for turning 'red war into redder' can never be silenced unless the majority wants it. Moreover, this task cannot be done either by God or religion as both seem devoid of power in modern times. It is true, man's life can be made harmonious in society only by his peaceful negotiations. Like Gautam Buddha, Hardy proposes the middle path for the solution of social conflicts. For this he says there must be a modest social and moral order of life in society for the welfare of mankind. He seems to think that man to make his life fruitful should harmonise his relationship with society, otherwise, his life becomes miserable. He affirms this by quoting Spencer's sarcastic statement : "The highest life (is) reached only when, besides helping to complete one another's lives by specified reciprocities of aid, men otherwise help to complete one another's lives."[17]

Even, existentialist thinkers criticise Social Darwinism for it excludes humanity and violates life-generating values like 'equality', 'liberty' and 'fraternity'. Moreover, it leads to 'misunderstanding' and 'social anarchy'. It is true that man's attachment to 'Social Darwinism' widens the gap between man and society, only to lead mankind to general extinction. Therefore, Hardy remarks; "Civilization .... an organism .... which if not surrounded with the proper conditions of life, will perish..."[18] Thus society which is based on disorder engages itself in constant killing and devising ways and means of torturing an individual.

After Nature and Society have deserted and condemned man to solitude and mental depression, the Hardyan protagonist considers whether religion and God can console and encourage his existence for the attainment of selfhood. But this never happens as both of them are meant to entangle him in other ways. Whatever little faith Hardy had as a child in conventional religion, he lost it once he read J.S. Mill, Charles Darwin, T.H. Huxley and Herbert Spencer. Supporting Hardy's loss of belief in God and Christianity, F.R. Southerington writes; "... the notion of life as a perpetual struggle for survival, with the down-treading of the weak or incapable, affected his outlook to such an extent that it contributed powerfully to the death in him of Christianity."[19] After his loss of faith, Hardy comes to the conclusion that the religion-oriented old way of life can never yield any positive values to man. To support this he quotes John Morley; "Religion, whatever destinies may be in store for it, is at least for the present hardly any longer an organic power. It is not that supreme, penetrating, controlling, decisive part of man's life."[20] Then what of the churches? Like Nietzsche, Hardy thinks, they are nothing but graves and gravestones of God. So, he concludes; "Religions are transitory and tentative, church of the future lies primarily in human breasts, and its teachings are there also."[21] Then what of God? Sartre, an atheist who defied even the beliefs of charity and goodness, claiming that both end in humiliating the receiver, said God was a useless and costly hypothesis. So is Nietzsche who declares; "God is dead. God remains dead. And we have killed him."[22] No doubt, Hardy records; " 'I have been looking for God for 50 years, and I think that if he had existed I should have discovered him'".[23]

The death of God, religion and allied beliefs is variously depicted in Hardy's poems, novels and short stories. His poems such as 'Hap' (WP) 'The Bedridden Peasant' (PPP) and 'New Year's Eve' (TL) show how the existence of God weakens man's hardihood and sense of responsibility without making his position secure, stable and endurable. Owing to this unbearable state of strife, Hardy never imagines life to be 'a pure delight, all gentle, true and just'. According to him, it is a thorny spot where men are made to live and are called to die and 'Life offers-to deny!' Hardy describes life's pending plan as one in which hopes dwindle, faiths waste away and none can change life as it is absurd and rootless. Therefore, he does not promise a happy and enduring life to an unborn generation :

> Vain vow ! No hint of mine may hence
> To theeward fly : to thy locked sense
>   Explain none can
>   Life's pending plan : (91)

In support of the view that man's life is a long labour in an indifferent society, Hardy quotes Victor Hugo; "He insists on the smallness of the personal element in life, the powerlessness of the human will in the face of inanimate forces such as superstition, society, or nature; dogmas, codes and things; religion, prejudice, or the elements... Man is not supreme, but a powerless unit in a crowd. Hugo's theme is the predestined fate of human existence the struggle between man and destiny; he insists upon the compulsion of circumstances, the tragic force that overrides the human will."[24]

Hardy's poem 'Childhood among the Ferns' expresses a sense of the burden of being alive and the pain of human need to act and be responsible in a world which is hostile to man :

> 'Why should I have to grow to man's estate,
> And this afar-noised World perambulate?' (846)

The sense of burden is also evident in his novels *Jude the Obscure* and *The Mayor of Casterbridge*, where Jude Fawley's son Little Father Time and Newson's daughter Elizabeth Jane respectively ask themselves as to why they were born in the world which was alien to them. The indifference of society to an individual is seen in one of his short stories where a character being afraid of society says; "....lack of human beings at night made me less fearful than the sight of them. Directly I saw a man's shape after dark in a lonely place I was frightened out of my senses."[25] This story is thematically similar to his poems 'In Tenebris' I, II and III and 'Wessex Heights'. However, Hardy endeavours to solve the problem of man's dislike for life in society by adopting 'stoic resignation' or 'an isolated way of life'. Upholding this J.H. Miller affirms; "The world is noise and glare, the threat of an engulfing violence which will shake and twist a man's life. Only if he can remain self-contained, sealed off from everything, can he escape his violence. He must therefore refuse any involvement in the world."[26]

Hardy's poems raise a number of different personal issues centring broadly around the conflict between an individual and community. His experience confirms; ".... how strange it is that we should talk so glibly of 'this cold world which shows no sympathy.' "[27] The conflict between an individual and society is explicitly stated in his poems, novels and short-stories. In these works, Hardy's protagonists suffer terribly though they have not wronged or corrupted or defrauded others. Indeed, on account of either his or society's lack of life sustaining values, man himself withdraws from society and leads a lonely life in mental isolation.

This aspect of society's insensibility, obduracy and frigidity to the painful existence of man is widely seen in the works of Sartre, Kafka, Camus and Dostoevsky, the existentialist writers. In Sartre's novel *Nausea* (1938), the hero, Roquention moves away from society after he felt the absurdity and inconsistency of life in it; while in Kafka's novel *The Trial* (1925), the hero, Josef K, suffers due to the erratic system of government. Similarly, in Camus' novel, *The Outsider*

(1942), the hero, Meursault remains in solitude and frustration because of the hostile social set-up; and in Dostoevsky's novel *Crime and Punishment* (1866), the hero, Raskolnikov rebels against the disconsolate world. In the works of all these great men of letters, man suffers mainly because of the erratic social order.

REFERENCES

1. Thomas Hardy, qt. by J.I.M. Stewart, *Thomas Hardy : A Critical Biography*, p. 42.
2. Thomas Hardy, *Literary Notes II*, Vol. II, p. 30.
3. Thomas Hardy, *Literary Notes I*, pp. 15-16.
4. Thomas Hardy, *Jude the Obscure*, preface VIII.
5. Thomas Hardy, *Jude the Obscure*, p. 284.
6. J.I.M. Stewart, *Thomas Hardy : A Critical Biography*, p. 22.
7. Thomas Hardy, *Literary Notes I*, Vol. I, p. 162.
8. Thomas Hardy, *Literary Notes I*, Vol. I, p. 150.
9. *Later Years*, p. 23.
10. Merryn Williams, *A Preface to Hardy*, p. 135.
11. *Life*, p. 406.
12. Karl Jaspers, qt. by G. Srinivasan, *Philosophical Perspective : East and West*, p. 39.
13. Martin Heidegger, qt. by G. Srinivasan, *Philosophical Perspectives*, p. 41.
14. Soren Kierkegaard, qt. by George Alfred Schrader, *Existential Philosophers*, p. 88.
15. J.S. Mill, qt. by Merryn Williams, *A Preface to Hardy*, p. 84.
16. Thomas Hardy, *Literary Notes I*, Vol. I, p. 149.
17. Spencer, qt. by Thomas Hardy, *Literary Notes I*, Vol. I., p. 163.
18. Thomas Hardy, *Literary Notes I*, Vol. I, pp. 217-218.
19. F.R. Southerington, *Hardy's Vision of Man*, p. 217.
20. John Morley, qt. by Thomas Hardy *Literary Notes II*, Vol. II, p. 123.
21. Thomas Hardy *Literary Notes II*, p. 104.
22. Friedrich Nietzsche, qt. by Robbin Alice Roth, "Nietzsche's Use of Atheism", reprinted in *International Philosophical Quarterly*, ed. by G.V. Potter, S.J., p. 53.
23. Thomas Hardy, qt. by J.G. Southworth, *The Poetry of Thomas Hardy*, p. 99.
24. Thomas Hardy, *Literary Notes I*, Vol. I, p. 169.
25. Thomas Hardy, *Stories and Poems of Thomas Hardy*, ed. by N.V. Meeres, p. 44.
26. J.H. Miller, *Thomas Hardy : Distance and Desire*, p. 6.
27. *Later Years*, p. 17.

5

Man and His own Self in Hardy's Poetry

> That we come to live, and are called to die.
> Yes, that's the thing
> In fall, in spring,
> That Yell'ham says :
> 'Life offers — to deny !
> ('Yell'ham-Wood's Story)

The moment both Nature and Society fail to support man, he starts seeking consolation in his own conscience, will-power and action. It is in his detachment both from Nature and Society he tries to make his life meaningful and authentic. However, it depends upon him whether he should achieve perfection in life with the help of the existing social order of life or again alienate himself from his self altogether. Man's solitary life in different social settings is depicted in several of Hardy's poems. Hardy's men and women who are isolated from society search for a new order of life in their own capacities. This demand them to make their life subjective and self-reliant. According to Jaspers, life is a possible reality which can reach comprehensible transcendence only through a final surrendering of reason. Although this position puts man under psychological tensions, it certainly induces him to lead a higher level of existence but in isolation. In this context, the subjective way of life of a solitary man acquires more importance. So Hardy states that "a 'sight for the finer qualities of existence, an ear for the still sad music of humanity are not to be acquired by the outer senses alone'; these aspects of life require a 'mental tactility that comes from a sympathetic appreciativeness of life in all its manifestations.' "[1]

In Hardy's view, human passions and virtues like love, faith, patience, enthusiasm, action, courage, confidence, hard work, a sense of responsibility and sacrifice animate and encourage an alienated man to a higher realm of life. This is also that what Kierkegaard thinks the more man thinks the less authentic he is. It is true that on account of objective way of life which is incomplete in itself, man cannot achieve anything great. George Alfred Schrader Jr. emphasises the importance of human passion when he asserts; "Human existence is an interest (*inter-esse*), an unrelieved and unceasing concern with the passion, the possibility, and the predicament of becoming oneself."[2] On the basis of these views one may conclude with a greater degree of certainty that man, an emotional being, may elevate himself only through a subjective way of life. However, the protagonists in Hardy's poems who succeed in attaining selfhood amidst their mental tumults are a minority, whereas those who fail to do so are many. In Hardy's poems, men and women who achieve self-realization in spite of their loneliness, despair, dread and difficulties are strong individuals. They are sublime in their virtues. They are right in their thought and choice; they are heroic in action; and they are responsible for their commitments good or ill. They are self-conscious and self-reliant. They neither care for nor need the help of the biological environment and society. David Perkins observes; ".... the protagonist almost always appears as a solitary, an outsider, or an individual alienated from the life of his fellows."[3] Besides, Hardyan protagonists devise various ways for their self-realization. They explore new roads of transcendence — roads which obviously assist them to become enlightened and independent.

This aspect of human life in mental isolation for the sake of self-preservation and self-realization is portrayed in some of Hardy's poems such as 'The Rover Come Home' and 'The Elopement'. In the first poem an adventurer travels from Canso Cape to Horn and East Indian Comorin. He discharges his duties as a solitary figure and achieves several things single-handed. His way of life denotes the strong possibility of attaining self-realization in solitude :

He has fought and bled in civil wars
Of no concern to him,

Has shot his fellows-beasts and men-
At risk of life and limb.
He has suffered fluxes, fevers,
Agues, and ills allied,
And now he's home. You look at him
As he talks by your fireside. (784)

An isolated man's life in society is also possible as may be seen in Hardy's poems. A narrative poem entitled 'The Elopement' reveals a determined maiden's strong earthy desire to elope with her lover in spite of immediate difficulties and consequent repercussions. She elopes with her paramour in order to be free from an arrested mode of life :

But in time convention won her, as it wins all women
at last,
And now she is rich and respectable, and time has
buried the past. (310)

The poems interpreted and assessed so far show man's existence free from an active attachment both with Nature and Society. They show how a man, who is ambitious, courageous, sincere and hardworking can find things which he wants. Indeed, man, if he is a determined and dedicated soul, can elevate himself to the position of Nietzschian superman.

On the other hand, people who have alienated themselves from society on account of their non-adjustment or maladjustment, lead a solitary life without any control over their self. In fact, they are a house divided against itself — contradictory and paradoxical. They are infirm in decision, split and disintegrated in personality and afraid of dread, despair and loneliness. They are neither able to console themselves in crisis nor capable of doing anything worthwhile. Nor are they able to revive their lost virtues and restore themselves to a good position which will liberate them from slavery either? They are ignorant, coward and unprincipled. They bring ruin on themselves. Kierkegaard calls such a man 'an imitation, a number, a cipher in the crowd' without any sense of realism in himself. According to him, this condition ".... at last leads him away from himself, so that he perishes in the dread."[4] Sartre calls him a man of *bad faith*, while Marcel says such man's life is like a 'dilapidated old house' or 'chronic rheumatism'. Similarly, Heidegger terms such man *Dasman* and Nietzsche *Helot*. In the view of these thinkers life without deep personal commitments is no life for an individual for the enrichment of his existence. For this they speak of 'inward hold' or an 'inward reflection' which is capable of at least carrying man on the threshold of realization. In the same manner, Hardy calls such man neither moral nor immoral but amoral, elsewhere as 'eccentric people' 'born out of due time', hence 'waiting in unhope' ('In Tenebris I'). Indeed, they lack a principled way of life, hence they remain beyond recovery. Hardy sympathetically asserts; "Why should a man's mind have been thrown into such close, sad, sensational, inexplicable relations with such a precarious object as his own body!"[5] In his view such man's life, unheroic and disintegrated, ends in self-alienation.

However, an alienated man, unsteady in nature, threatened by anxiety, dread, anguish and nothingness remains in psychic tensions. This is because of his emotional conflicts between his inner conscience and outer actions which ultimately disintegrate his mode of survival. Additionally it weakens his sense of stability, harmony and conscience in proportion to its vigour and intensity. Ultimately the suicidal condition tends to reduce him to a state of *Dasman* or *Helot*. In existentialist ethic, the people who are termed *Dasman* or *Helot* are sunk into an inauthentic mode of existence because of their primordial conflict between their inner conscience and outer commitments. Their life is essentially characterized by vices like negligence, indulgence, cruelty, hostility, despair, dread and obduracy. In a sense, their heart and soul are degenerated to such an extent that they are beyond recovery. Their utter inability to achieve things which they desire leads them to an everlasting despair. Thus man's failure to achieve a harmonious sexual, personal and social relationship culminates in his utter self-alienation.

The theme of self-alienation which is variously called in existentialism as self-suppression, self-idealization and self-anaesthesia is clearly depicted in Hardy's poems such as 'The Impercipient' (WP), 'A Broken Appointment', 'Tess's Lament' (PPP) and 'The Orphaned Old Maid' (TL). In them the desires of Hardyan protagonists are left unfulfilled despite their desperate struggle. Their ambition to do this or that and possess or realize something in society is wholly marred by their own faults, absurdities and conflicts. The prime reason for this, Hardy thinks, is the fate which disrupts and defeats human efforts. It is fate, an incomprehensible power that drags human beings into a mire of doom and disaster. Furthermore, it demoralizes man's soul and heart and destroys his passions connected with the process of regeneration.

Hardy's poem, 'The Impercipient' clearly states the theme of man's self-alienation. Here Hardy presents the visionary experience without faith. The poem seems to be centrally the poet's defence against attacks prompted by his sombre expression and outlook and it gives a religious colouring to the solace which he is deprived of. It shows the protagonist's helplessness, susceptibility and disintegration of personality. Man's self-consciousness which is his *elan vital* (life force) of the mind in action is being disrupted. Hence, he becomes a split-personality. In the poem the dilemma is that the speaker is always blind to the sights his 'brethren see'. Besides, he cannot find the joys his comrades do :

> That with this bright believing band
> I have no claim to be,
> That faiths by which my comrades stand
> Seem fantasies to me,
> And mirage-mists their Shining Land,
> Is a strange destiny

This is a mystery which consigns the protagonist to infelicity. The poem carries the implication into a metaphor :

> I am like a gazer who should mark
> An inland company
> Standing upfingered, with, 'Hark ! hark !
> The glorious distant sea !'
> And feel, 'Alas, 'tis but yon dark
> And wind-swept pine to me! (44)

The stanza seems to express the protagonist's as well as Hardy's malady, that is, the sense of being cut off from his fellow human beings. In this connection, in his essay 'Hardy and the Poetry of Isolation', David Perkins remarks; "Throughout the poem, and especially in the image of a "bird deprived of wings", there is nostalgia for the beliefs and impressions which give joy to other people, a wanting to share them, and a feeling that he cannot. And the pathos is not weakened by the suggestion that the speaker's vision may be truer — the nostalgia and the isolation are still present."[6] The protagonist is unable to come out of an arrested mode of existence, because he is a self-alienated person. Similarly, in the poem 'A Broken Appointment', a devoted lover impatiently awaits a married woman whom he likes most in spite of her dislike for him. He remembers her help to him in his hour of crisis. Anyway, she does not come and his agony becomes so intense that he longs to see her thinking that 'love alone can lend loyalty'. But his misunderstanding her absence simply leads him to wait in 'unhope' — a sort of 'self-alienation'.

In another case, there are two betrothed women who are neglected by their husbands. Nevertheless, their misery and suffering is not alleviated either by Nature or by Society. They are depicted in 'She, to Him' sonnet series and 'Tess's Lament'. In 'She, to Him', a wedded woman worries that her beauty has been faded and she has been neglected by her husband for another love, whereas, in the second poem, 'Tess's Lament', a woman who is recently married suffers because of her confession. Here Tess the protagonist repents :

> And it was I who did it all
>   Who did it all;
> 'Twas I who made the blow to fall
>   On him who thought no guile.

She wishes that her memories be blotted, every relic be obliterated and all graces be banished. Hence, Tess fallen from the grace of her husband, resolves not to be in the hostile world where some incomprehensible forces ultimately control her life without any regard to her wishes :

> Well, it is finished-past, and he
> Has left me to my misery,
>
> And I must take my Cross on me
>   For wronging him awhile. (141)

Tess is a rare woman who plays out her passionate part under the shadow of Fate that does not care whether she suffers or rejoices. Assessing her character, Harold Child says; "Her fineness and clarity of spirit, her faith and devotion, her strength and tenacity in love, her essential sweetness, compel the reader to share the author's anguish of pity for her sorrows, his passionate indignation at the stupid waste of her lovely qualities."[7] The conflict between her inner consciousness and outer commitments leads her to an eternal conflict which culminates in crime and consequent execution. This may rightly be called her 'self-alienation'.

The poem 'The Orphaned Old Maid' too shares the same human agony and tone though different in theme. The protagonist, an orphaned woman, regrets having obeyed her father to remain unmarried until his death. Her action much against her wishes on account of her ignorance ruins her. Though she is not a bad woman, she fails to fulfil her individual destiny. People like Tess and the orphaned old woman who are not wise enough to choose and act correctly fail to elevate themselves to the position of authentic mode of existence. Hence, they continue in a bereaved situation which is a kind of abandonment of human existence. In these poems, particularly, 'She, to Him' and 'The Orphaned Old Maid', there is a frequent recurrence of the thought of old age as a destroyer of physical beauty and thereby undermining the dignity of woman in the view of man.

Male counterparts of self-alienation are pictured in poems like 'The Revisitation' and 'A Poor Man and a Lady'. The protagonists pictured here struggle to achieve transcendental bliss through their love and companionship. But their attempts end in abortion on account of their own individual limitations. In the first poem a man persuades a woman he likes to marry him despite her unwillingness to marry him because of his poverty. Similarly, in 'A Poor Man and a Lady' an aristocratic lady rejects a poor man.

The theme of self-suppression is evident in Hardy's poems 'How She Went to Ireland' (WW) and 'The Beauty' (LLE). In the first poem a desolate woman frustrated by the absurdity of life migrates to Ireland, whereas in the second, a beautiful lady, Miss Verry, is unhappy with her beauty because her personal attractions have been misunderstood by others :

> I hate my beauty in the glass :
> My beauty is not I :
> I wear it : one cares whether, alas,
> Its wearer live or die! (572)

Since, man is not in perfect harmony with his fellow-beings either because of his limitations or because of social codes, he does not think that 'love' will provide him happiness. Poems like 'Revulsion' and 'Neutral Tones' (WP) portray the theme that 'love' cannot become an eternal means of self-realization. It is always mixed with hatred and indifference. Though formerly love was man's serious concern, it has now ceased to be a joy and bliss. Therefore, Hardy accuses the modern age of joyless wisdom : "*The Passion of love* invariably drives men and women to an extreme step in one direction or another. It will send some to the Cloister, some to the Tribune, some to the Stage, some to heroism, some to crime, and all to their natural calling".[8] That is why, in the poem, 'I Said to Love' (PPP) Hardy in his mood of anger accepts the extinction of mankind if it is not possible without love. In his love poems we see lovers or married partners not in perfect harmony with each other on account of their decay of love, disillusion, severance, incompatibility and inconstancy. There is the theme of unhappiness striking. But this is not on account of Hardy's bitter experience in married life. Regarding this James G. Southworth says; "So much for one phase of Hardy's treatment of love. It is clear that he did not write from an embittered heart. No one had a deeper respect for the finest aspects of love than did he. No one was more careful to preserve its bloom and rare flavor.[9]

In existentialism this state of life is called "the bereaved situation of human existence."[10] Such bereaved men are weak, fragile and helpless as nobody cares for them in society. However, they may become good only by their virtue of sincerity and hard working. Hardy says; "It is the man who bases his action upon what the world is thinking, no matter what it may be saying, who rises to the top."[11] According to him, man, a free and conscious being, may create his own values and attain self-realization. Sartre thinks man by creating a new moral and social order of life, may lead a full and purposive existence in this purposeless universe. Accordingly, man invested with freedom and responsibility sometimes strives to create his own values and attain perfection. But in course of trials and tribulations he is rather misled, disturbed and defeated. This kind of man's unworthy struggle for existence is based on his indulgence and negligence. Therefore, existentialists think that this state of human life is based on man's gross ignorance. This kind of man's self-alienation is depicted in Hardy's poem 'The Two Men'. Here two companions who studied in the same school and were shaped by common rules, are ambitious and adventurous. They are also equal in age, wit, status and strength. In this situation one of the two aspires for a higher level of life :

> 'I'll brace to higher aims', said he,
> 'I'll further Truth and Purity;
> Thereby to mend the mortal lot
> And sweeten sorrow....

But he fails to become an ideal man which he had planned to become earlier. His failure to stand for high ideals demoralizes him altogether :

> Once done, his soul was so betossed,
> It found no more the force it lost;

Hope was his only drink and food,
And hope extinct, decay ensued.

Meanwhile, his friend equally ambitious, devises various ways to find his way to fortune. He desires to become rich and respectable. But he too fails to do the 'deed so joyously hailed', for he wanted to 'live by doing nought'. So his 'projects are wholly marred'. Thus gloom and want oppress him hard and he meets the fate of his friend :

....., living to so mean an end,
Whereby he'd lost his every friend,
He perished in the pauper sty
When his old mate lay dying nigh. (50)

Here one friend ignores practical aspects of life because of his high ideals, and the other is a lazy dreamer. They are not dedicated to a purpose, hence, little by little, they are striped of everything : position, means, respect and love. They go down gradually till they become lonely and bereft. The poem is tragic and bitter but in it we see how human desire and endeavour are thwarted by the irony of circumstance.

Hardy, an evolutionary meliorist admires the ambitious life of these two friends, but he does not like their negligence. He calls this their 'internal conflict'. He writes about the situation of such persons : "... You may regard a throng of people as containing a certain small minority who have sensitive souls; .... you divide them into the mentally unquickened, mechanical, soulless, and the living, throbbing, suffering, vital. In other words, into souls and machines."[12] Here 'souls' is meant something worthy and authentic, whereas, 'machines', something unmeritorious and undistinguished. The former position leads man to an authentic mode of existence where man is less villainous and more human. In fact, he occupies a position where he could afford to be himself, to create and live by himself. Whereas, the position of machines leads man to an inauthentic mode of existence where he will be more inhuman and dishonest. And in him there is some vital weakness and radical ineffectuality that lead to his self-alienation.

As a creative artist Hardy displays human reality in its bareness and frankness. His poetry being his own impression of life, reflects human life in varied social settings. His sincere portrayal of man's psychological and moral tensions discloses an individual's suffering in loneliness which is hardly relieved by human love and compassion. But Hardy regrets his protagonist's frequent failure to get consolation and contentment even when he is honest, docile, hard working and a mute sufferer. This grim state of man is evident in his poems 'Wessex Heights' and 'In Tenebris' I, II and III. In the first poem Hardy portrays the state of mind of a man who is estranged from the hostile world. The poem reveals his bereaved situation in its entirety. The solitary figure who is haunted by his memory meditates over his personal crises while he is wandering over the Wessex heights which represents his active separation from the belligerent society. However he is meditating over the past in order to regenerate his life, his spirit is weakened :

> Nobody sees it but I, and it makes my breast beat
> out of tune. (261)

Assessing the poem, Prof. J.H. Miller writes; ".... the speaker is a memory-haunted victim of his failure to love; his movement from the lowlands to the heights represents withdrawal in fear and disgust into the emptiness of his own mind."[13]

The theme is enlarged in 'In Tenebris' I, II and III. These lyrical poems start with Latin mottoes displaying the tragic condition of human life in the face of glaring misfortunes. In the first poem, Hardy depicts an isolated man's meekness and weakness. The short lines of the poem emphasize the tragic situation of his personal life. The bereaved man pictured here does not suffer from doubts for he has no hopes. The title of the lyric, 'In Tenebris' means 'in the darkness' and it suggests a life that has no aspirations. Moreover, the Latin motto meaning " 'My heart is smitten, and withered like grass' "[14] denotes the frailty and futility of human strife. Even Nature appears bleak and degenerated, but the man does not mind it, for his very head and heart are still bleaker and more demoralized. The climatic phrase 'waits in unhope' is the very embodiment of his 'self-alienation'.

The second lyric however different in style and versification, follows the first in theme. The hostile world seems a nightmare to the protagonist here. Nevertheless, he does not accuse it as a bad place but he complains that it has evil and oddities. Besides, he says happiness is not accessible to man, for it is largely destroyed by 'crookedness, custom, and fear'. Similarly he thinks, if 'way to the better there be, it exacts a full look at the worst'. Hence, he resolves not to be there any more :

> The blot seems straightway in me alone; one better
> he were not here

.... I am one born out of due time, who has not
calling here. (137)

The poem carries the desire of the protagonist not to live any more. This is expanded again in the third poem where the world appears a welter of futile doings. Therefore, the poet asserts that man's accumulated knowledge will not be helpful in his hour of crisis :

...vision could vex or that knowledge could numb, (138)

This lyrical poem, according to Douglas Brown and Kenneth Marsden, is connected with man's loss and bereavement. As a whole, these lyrics of the name 'In Tenebris' are pictures of man's self-alienation in their entirety. Hardy, like his contemporary, A.E. Housman, has depicted the sorriest aspects of human existence. His poems display man's self-crisis in their varied facets.

Another problem which arises in the context of existentialist ethic is the lack of human solidarity which unfailingly mars man's attainment of self-realization. Supporting the view, Kierkegaard maintains; "To exist is to be an individual; the abstract does not exist; and to be an individual is to choose and to be impassioned. Thus, existence is the moment of free and passionate decision; and as interpreted ontologically, this moment marks the liberty of man to will the good and the perfect."[15] It is true, individuality is the life force or *elan vital* for the attainment of self-hood. Nietzsche too supports this, when he emphasizes on man's action, and responsibility. Similarly, Sartre in his work *'L' Existentialisme est un humanisme* (1946) insists on the issue of action and involvement in life. He asserts; "Man comes into existence for himself and brings the world into existence for himself by the ceaseless separation and projection of himself."[16] Here by 'individualist' is meant not a selfish and greedy person anxious to satisfy his appetites, but a man of distinct personality who will definitely try to attain fulfilment. In the words of D.H. Lawrence. "He is a man who, being beyond the average, chooses to rule his own life to his own completion."[17] In this regard, conscience, freedom, choice, action and responsibility which constitute the concept of individuality are emphasized for the completion of meaningful life. If these qualities are absent in man, he will be termed a *Dasman*, or a *Helot* or 'an imitation, a mere number in a crowd'. Therefore, Sartre insists on the necessity of authenticity to an individual to lead a heroic mode of life. But he does not answer the question why man should pursue authentic mode of existence especially when the alternative, *i.e.*, inauthentic mode of life is more attractive and easy.

Whatever may be the ethic, the necessity of possessing individuality is more essential to become an authentic existent. As D.H. Lawrence, an existentialist writer thinks, individuality is a must in order to be or become himself. It is a necessary element for man's eternal fascination. Both Hardy and existentialist thinkers separately arrive at a similar conclusion that man sinks into an arrested mode of life in case he fails to be right in his choice and heroic in his action. It is true, life devoid of individuality becomes absurd and meaningless. Moreover, conflicts between passions and choice, choice and action and action and responsibility bring man disasters. So Hardy quotes J.J. Rousseau that : "A man without energy or any moral worth beyond a personal good nature is useless for any social end."[18]

The inauthentic mode of human life is closely related to the theme of absurdity. This is shown in Hardy's poems 'At a Country Fair' and 'Fragment'. In the first, a giant physically handicapped and mentally retarded is chased by a dwarf in a Western country fair. Hardy, the narrator observes that though the giant is physically stronger, he is not aware of it as if he were a man of no 'independent mind' or 'will' of any kind. Hence :

> Wherever the dwarf decided to go
> At his heels the other trotted meekly, (451)

In this absurd pantomime, we may see man's life meaningless and degenerated. This tragedy shows the reason why mankind has to write its history everyday, and why man's life is often at the verge of disaster and extinction. The other poem, 'Fragment' displays the absurdity of life in a different manner. Here, two solitary figures almost unconscious of their surroundings, live a meaningless life. The poem reveals the victims' feelings of fear, anguish and nothingness. Moreover the manner of eccentricity, neurotic expression, ambiguity, tumult and moral and mental tensions have been found an outlet throughout these inauthentic existents. As a whole, the poem stands for the absurd life of modern man :

> 'The sense of waiting here strikes strong;
> Everyone's waiting, waiting, it seems to me;
> What are you waiting for so long?-
> What is to happen?' I said.

His companion's answer is that of pure ignorance :

> 'O we are waiting for one called God,' said they,
> '(Though by some the Will, or Force, or Laws;

And, vaguely, by some, the Ultimate Cause);
Waiting for him to see us before we are clay.
Yes; waiting, waiting, for God *to know it*'... (464)

For the further question as to what they want to know from God, they reply that they are waiting to know how things happen and by whose strange laws. Thinking these people as eccentric, Hardy writes; "The eccentric person only gets out of the main stream of life to float in shallow water (which the masses have seen, considered, and avoided)."[19]

An inner conflict and disintegration in the heart of an individual reveal *bad faith (Mauvaise Foi)* though it is not a perversion but a split in the sub-consciousness. The development of dread and nothingness makes human existence largely trouble-torn. The endless dichotomy and susceptibility of man's life is reflected in Hardy's later poems like 'Nature's Questioning' and 'Memory and I'. Here in the first poem a man suffers in loneliness and dread. He is an alienated individual unrelieved by human compassion. In this situation, he wonders why he has been placed in a world of futile doing where life and death are near neighbours :

We wonder, ever wonder, why we find us here!
'Has some Vast Imbecility,
Mighty to build and blend,
But impotent to tend,
Framed us in jest, and left us now to hazardry?

Helplessly he concludes :

Thus things around. No answerer I....
Meanwhile the winds, and rains,
And Earth's old glooms and pains
Are still the same, and Life and Death are
neighbours nigh. (43)

Similarly, in 'Memory and I' there is an everlasting conflict between the protagonist's 'memory and 'reality'. Here the protagonist is obsessed with his past. Consequently, he asks his memory whether it will bring him any joy and solace. On the contrary, his memory answers that as human truth has been crumbled and human joy, hope and faith have gone, it cannot provide him any joy and bliss. However, the speaker asks his memory whether, at least, he will get human love and compassion :

'O Memory, where is now my love,

That rayed me as a God above?'

But his hope crumbles when his memory reveals the fact :

'I saw her in an ageing shape
Where beauty used to be;
That her fond phantom lingers there
Is only known to me.' (150)

The lyric shows the protagonist's self-alienation on account of his inner conflicts. On a close inspection of this all of Hardy's works becomes clear, that is his interest in the past. He dwells much upon memories, and often with sympathy. It is in his memories, we see his, or his protagonist's love for wine, woman and dance, or his memory of the church music, or his memory of kith and kin and dear ones.

Hardy calls this 'bereaved situation of human life' as 'helplessness', 'worthlessness' and 'fallenness'. In existentialism, this is referred to as *intense psychological trauma* or "Alienation in its most active form-the rejection of being oneself at the attempt to become the other, the ideal self".[20] Furthermore, an alienated man wholly ruined by his own designs can hardly recover his original position and become an authentic being. He looks a drunkard addicted to his habit of drinking. Sartre compares such *Dasman* or *Helot* to gamblers. According to him; "It is that of a gambler who had freely and sincerely decided not to gamble any more and who on approaching the gambling table, suddenly sees all his resolutions melt away."[21]

However, an individual who is fallen from grace can also become an authentic man if he improves the quality of his life. He suffers not because of others but because of his own limitations. If he overcomes weaknesses he can attain fulfilment. In fact, self-alienation is not a grave danger to his primordial existence in relation to his transcendence. He may adjust with his self, society and biological environment so much so that he may ensure the process of his self-purification and realization.

REFERENCES

1. Thomas Hardy, *The Science of Fiction*, ed. by L.A. Bjork, Vol. I, Intro., p. XXIX.
2. George Alfred Schrader Jr. *Existential Philosophers.*, p. 88.
3. David Perkins, 'Hardy and the Poetry of Isolation' ed. by A.J. Guerard, *Hardy : A Collection of Critical Essays,* p. 143.
4. Kierkegaard, qt. by Lakshmi Saxena, *Encounter with Transcendence*, p. 17.

5. Thomas Hardy, qt. by M.D. Zabel, 'Hardy in Defense of His Art', ed. by A.J. Guerard, *Hardy : A Collection of Critical Essays*, p. 33.
6. David Perkins, 'Hardy and the Poetry of Isolation' ed. by A.J. Guerard, *Hardy : A Collection of Critical Essays*, pp. 155-156.
7. Harold Child, *Thomas Hardy*, p. 67.
8. Robert Orange, qt. by Thomas Hardy, *Literary Notes II*, p. 96.
9. James G. Southworth, *The Poetry of Thomas Hardy*, p. 38.
10. R.A. Sinari, *Contemporary Existentialism-its limitations*, p. 63.
11. *Early Life*, p. 16.
12. *Life*, pp. 185-186.
13. J.H. Miller, qt. by F.R. Giordano, 'Hardy's Farewell to Fiction' ed. by James Gibson and Trevor Johnson, *Thomas Hardy Poems*, p. 253.
14. James Gibson, *The Complete Poems of Thomas Hardy*, p. 958.
15. Kierkegaard, qt. by R.A. Sinari, *Contemporary Existentialism-its limitations*, pp. 24-25.
16. J.P. Sartre, qt. by H.J. Blackham, *Six Existentialist Thinkers*, p. 147.
17. D.H. Lawrence, 'Hardy's Predilection d' artiste', ed. by A.J. Guerard, *Hardy : A Collection of Critical Essays*, pp. 40-50.
18. J.J. Rousseau, qt. by Thomas Hardy, *Literary Notes I*, p. 707.
19. Thomas Hardy, *Literary Notes I*, p. 109.
20. F.A. Weiss, *Self-Alienation* ed. by Eric and Mary Josephson, pp. 468-469.
21. J.P. Sartre, qt. by John Macquarrie, *Existentialism*, p. 170.

6

Quest for Selfhood in Hardy's Poetry

New thoroughfares in sad humanity for transcendence

The analysis of Hardy's poetry shows man's withdrawal from his biological environment, society and his own self in quest of selfhood. In the course of their struggle for perfection, Hardyan men find sustenance in their strong will-power and determination to act. They exercise their freedom of choice with a sense of commitment, striving to attain self-hood. But their struggle for self-realization does not run smooth as it is beset with difficulties in the world. In the course of their struggle, Hardyan characters try to overcome their moral conflicts in order to harmonise their life — the quality of thought, nature of choice, style of action and sense of responsibility. As a result, they become more conscious, heroic and responsible adopting a proper way of action. But they never desire to submit themselves to the surrounding forces either in Nature or in Society. Hardy's men live in the world with a sense of 'stoic-resignation' which is similar to Albert Camus' concept of 'lucid-indifference'. In spite of their agitations, Hardy's protagonists never follow the traditional way of life or the beaten track of religion. They are aware of their drawbacks and they do not aspire for something that is beyond their means. Since they are guided by their conscience and work sincerely, their future lies entirely in their own hands. They can either make or mar their life too. But they submit entirely to their innate selves to achieve peace and enlightenment. In short they try to overcome their self-alienation. This aspect of the Hardyan protagonist's enlightened vision is evident in several of his poems. For evidence 'Wessex Heights' shows a forlorn man's peaceful life on his favourite heights.

The poem shows how a man frustrated in life can get joy and solace amidst his environment. Here a memory-haunted figure, wandering on the heights meditating over the past is much happier and freer from the 'phantoms of the plain' as the calm and clear atmosphere is spiritually comfortable. A kind of Wordsworthian benevolence of Nature is evident here :

> So I am found on Ingpen Beacon, or on Wylls-Neck
> to the west,
> Or else on homely Bulbarrow, or little Pilsdon Crest,
> Where men have never cared to haunt, nor women have
> walked with me,
> And ghosts then keep their distance; and I know some
> liberty. (261)

A happy human life based on 'stoic-resignation' is seen in Hardy's nature poems 'On a Fine Morning', 'An August Midnight', 'The Darkling Thrush', 'The Milkmaid', 'From Her in the Country', 'Let Me Enjoy', 'Weathers' and 'Great Things'. In these poems, Hardy thinks that co-existence is possible for man amidst Nature if he is willing to live with her. According to him, 'Man-Nature' relationship based on love, veneration, regard and reciprocity may lead him to fruitful life. So man may live amidst Nature's setting and he may make his life endurable. But Hardy cannot help quoting Aristotle that man should not depend on Nature for everything as she herself is imperfect. He should simply make her a true companion, for he is a product of her milieux. In this regard, E.R. Oxford's observation is striking; "Man is held to be a part of Nature, a product of the definite and orderly evolution which is universal" and, "It is his destiny to understand and control it".[1] Another critic, D.R. Bhandari maintains; "Man is not alien to Nature in spite of its working against his plans and projects."[2]

The poem 'On a Fine Morning', establishes the fact that man is a part of Nature and the latter is meant for his survival :

> But as nothing other than
> Part of a benignant plan;
> Proof that earth was made for man. (93)

The poem undoubtedly shows the primitive spirit that 'man' and 'Nature' are not alien to each other in spite of their differences. Similar is the theme of 'An August Midnight'. The man portrayed in the poem seems to be a writer who is visited by various creatures as he sits writing at night. His communion with creatures assures him joy and solace, as they reveal him the mystery of Nature that is unknown to human beings :

> On this scene enter-winged, horned, and spined-
> A longlegs, a moth, and a dumbledore;
> While 'mid my page there idly stands
> A sleepy fly, that rubs its hands.....
>
> Thus meet we five, in this still place,
> At this point of time, at this point in space.
> — My guests besmear my new-penned line,
> Or bang at the lamp and fall supine.
> 'God's humblest, they!' I muse. Yet why?
> They know Earth-secrets that know not I. (113)

Another poem in a similar spirit which has attracted a large number of readers and admirers is 'The Darkling Thrush'. The poem which reveals the mysteries of present, past and future was written at the turn of 19th century bringing for posterity hopes and inspiration which were absent in the monotonous and chaotic life of 19th century. This lyric was inspired by P.B. Shelley's 'To a Skylark' and John Keats' 'Ode to a Nightingale'. Hardy seems to think that these birds have revealed the mysteries of happier worlds to the respective poets who were disillusioned by pain, misery and suffering around them. Similarly, the 'thrush' aged, frail, gaunt and small 'in blast-beruffled plume' looks obviously born for death. The scene moves Hardy, the poet to prophecy, so he thinks it is not an ordinary bird, but a bird which knows more than man. John Keats in his 'Ode' wishes to leave the world and fade away into the happier world of the bird for getting highest bliss. Likewise, P.B. Shelley feels that the 'Skylark' is much in a happier condition than he is. Likewise Hardy thinks the 'Thrush' though weak in body is happy and ecstatic as it knows 'some blessed Hope' which he does not know. The fervourless protagonist of the poem hears somewhere a full-hearted 'thrush' singing joyfully to announce new hopes and aspirations to the new century :

> At once a voice arose among
> The bleak twigs overhead
> In a full-hearted evensong
> Of joy illimited;
> . . . .

Some blessed Hope, whereof he knew
And I was unaware. (119)

The poem is autobiographical so far it reveals Hardy's personal crises around 1900. He was disgraced by the invidious critics upon the publication of his novels *Tess of the d' Urbervilles* and *Jude the Obscure*. Secondly, he was unhappy in his married life with Emma Hardy. Finally, he was not satisfied with the order of life of his age which was disharmonious.

It is striking as it closely reflects Hardy's vision. W.H. Auden and Dylan Thomas, Hardy's followers, admired it. The former remarks; "To see the individual life related not only to the local social life of its time, but to the whole of human history, life on the earth, the stars, gives one both humility and self-confidence".[3] Auden thinks as the difference between an individual and Nature is so slight, man should reconcile himself to her and work for his evolution. In Tom Paulin's view 'The Darkling Thrush' is similar to John Keats' 'Ode to Nightingale' ('The weariness, the fever and the fret') and Matthew Arnold's 'Dover Beach' ('turbid ebb and flow of human misery'). Indeed, at a close glance, Hardy's poetry is of an agnostic humanist's but not of a puritanical Christian's.

Man's harmonious co-existence with Nature is still deep in the poem 'The Milkmaid' where the under-currents of joy and pain of a milkmaid in the beautiful natural phenomenon are shown. She is not only a companion to Nature but also a true part of it. Like the life of Deggory Venn of Hardy's novel *Far from the Madding Crowd*, her life is peaceful. Her virtues like simplicity, nobility and sacrifice make her an authentic individual. The poem reveals the feminine power, grace and presence of both the milkmaid and Nature :

Upheaves and falls; the milk purrs in the pail;
Few pilgrims but would choose
The peace of such a life in such a vale.
The maid breathes words - to vent,
It seems, her sense of Nature's scenery,
Of whose life, sentiment,
And essence, very part itself is she. (126)

A woman in 'From Her in the Country' speculates that life in beautiful countrysides is more harmonious than in 'Crass clanging town'. Here her very annoyance due to the commercialization of life ('city din and sin') finds an expression :

I said : How beautiful are these flowers, this wood,
One little bud is far more sweet to me
Than all man's urban shows; and then I stood
Urging new zest for bird, and bush, and tree; (187)

Man's benevolent intercourse with Nature is shown in the poem 'Weathers'. Here man is shown in perfect harmony with his biological milieu. He is a companion of his fellow-beings and also of birds, beasts and trees. Truly he is part of the very weather in which he lives :

This is the weather the cuckoo likes,
    And so do I;
When showers betumble the chestnut spikes,
    And nestlings fly :
And the little brown nightingale bills his best,
And they sit outside at 'The Travellers' Rest',
And maids come forth sprig-muslin drest,
And citizens dream of the south and west,
    And so do I. (512)

The poem illustrates an important fact that man's love of Nature is not for profit but for pleasure, harmony and fulfilment. The protagonist's love of Nature is simple but noble and spiritual. In fact, he loves Nature to find grace and solace. This aspect of human love and veneration for natural phenomena is still deep in 'Let Me Enjoy' and 'Great Things'. In the first poem, man accepts life in all its grey and green hues. Though the earth has other aim than his delight he resolves to make Nature a companion for her benevolence and gracious presence :

LET me enjoy the earth no less
Because the all-enacting Might
That fashioned forth its loveliness. (193)

Just the same, the protagonist of the second poem, 'Great Things' loves Nature as he loves Wine and Woman :

O cyder is a great thing,
A great thing to me!
. . . .
O dancing is a great thing,
A great thing to me!
. . . .

O love is, yes, a great thing,
A great thing to me!
. . . .
Will these be always great things,
Great things to me? . . . .
Let it befall that One will call,
'Soul, I have need of thee :'
What then? Joy-jaunts, impassioned flings,
Love, and its ecstasy,
Will always have been great things,
Great things to me! (414)

In these poems particularly 'Weathers', 'Let Me Enjoy' and 'Great Things', a kind of Wordsworthian benevolence to human beings is shown. Here man's love for Nature leads to his love of fellow human beings. For instance, the love of the protagonist of the poem 'Great Things' for natural objects like wine (cyder) leads to his love of dance and woman. So he thinks human love is greater than all the things. This is explicit in the last stanza of the poem. No wonder, 'Great Things' and 'Let Me Enjoy' bear direct witness to man's pleasure in the simple sensuous joys of the world of Nature. These are also autobiographical poems where the poet expresses the delight of his early life. On account of his optimism expressed in poems like these, Hardy is considered not a life-denier. His theory of human reality as expressed in his poetry shows man's interest in evolution in every shape and sound. Supporting Hardy's optimism, Jean Brooks asserts; "Only a man who loved life in every fibre of his being could feel so keenly the betrayal of its potentialities in the sight of a starving thrush, a blinded bird, or an unwanted pauper child".[4]

These poems reflect man's special love, and regard for Nature on account of her gracious presence, spiritual awakening and stability. Nature in them has been shown a divine power and personality for the progressive redemption of those who live with her. Hardy thinks every part of Nature is indispensable for the enrichment of human virtues and human existence on the earth is hardly possible without Nature. As Hardy's knowledge and experience of life matured, his view of, and attitude towards life underwent considerable changes. His attitude towards life became more humane. He considered Nature's flora and fauna as inseparable parts of man's living. Like Romantic poets he thinks Nature is not alien to man in spite of her neutralism and occasional malignity. Our close study of Hardy's pastoral poetry reveals the fact that man's life is possible and fruitful only in his environment primarily in consonance with natural objects. In fact, everyone's life in the country is absolutely dependent on woods, air, earth, sky, sun, rain, snow, wind, dawn, darkness, seasons and so on. The natural entities for him are the masters, acquaintances, personal assistants and instructors. Similarly Jaspers feels the indispensability of Nature for man. In his opinion man in order to lead a peaceful and creative existence, should live like lower animals without any rivalry or conflicts. This view is implicit in Hardy's 'The Darkling Thrush' and 'An August Midnight' quoted above. In these poems, Hardy recognises the joy and thrill the humblest creatures have which is beyond the reason of human sense and intellect. If we subjectively analyse Hardy's Nature poems, we cannot help comparing him to Jaspers and Ponty the believers in Nature's benevolence. It is only another matter that he exposed the drawbacks of Nature on account of her lack of an adequate system.

On another level, Hardyan protagonists realize their mistakes and reconcile themselves with society. They resolve to co-exist with their fellow beings with a view to enriching their social relationships. Whatever may be the aftermath, they turn to others for love, compassion, contentment and solidarity. Of course they have to experience inner 'dread', '*angst*' (anxiety or mental neurosis) and 'nothingness' on account of their reconciliation with the broader community. They readjust with the society and sacrifice certain desires in expectation of mutual benefit or common betterment. In other words, this is called their 'social service' or 'sacrifice' in a broader sense. But this kind of life requires higher virtues like suffering, sacrifice, endurance, simplicity and nobility.

This way of life amidst society has another dimension. It involves co-existence with people of different nature and distinction. Therefore an individual in society must have virtues like love, respect, reciprocity and sacrifice. He should be right in his way of life and style of functioning. Moreover, he should be aware of the limits of his freedom, his sense of duty and responsibility. This mode of 'Man-Society' relationship with a view of an individual's rational and enlightened progress in society has been depicted on two planes in Hardy's poems. On the first, there is 'Man-Woman' relationship, and on the second, 'Man-Society' relationship.

As far as 'Man-Woman' relationship is concerned, human love, faith, mercy, forgiveness, sacrifice and willingness play a significant role. In fact, these virtues become a kind of guidelines for the establishment of 'Man-Woman's' personal and sexual relationship. This is shown in 'Ditty' and 'The Dance at the Phoenix'. The first poem is one of Hardy's most lovely and homely of the heart-stirring shorter lyrics dedicated to his wife Emma. It evinces a happy life of two true souls. The refrain 'where she dwells' produces an atmosphere at once cheerful and gracious. Here Hardy's protagonist uses love as the most elementary passion for transcendental bliss. His protagonist's love and romance have found their cathartic expression. Hence the poem evidences the spiritual power and healing spirit of love and it ends in a philosophical note :

Upon that fabric fair
    'Here is she!'
Seems written everywhere
    Unto me.

He feels he is lucky to have got such a companion who is lovely and gracious :

And Devotion droops her glance
    To recall
What bond — servants of Chance
    We are all.

I but found her in that, going
On my errant path unknowing,
I did not out-skirt the spot
That no spot in earth excels,
— Where she dwells! (18)

Ernest Brennecke Jr., commenting on this lyric says; "It is a poem that does not suffer by comparison with the best of Wordsworth's Lucy poems ('She dwelt among Untrodden Ways') though the touch of pathos is lacking."[5] The poem 'The Dance at the Phoenix' also expresses something about special love which can become a means of ensuring mutual awakening and stability. It is about a soldier's love story in which Hardy dwells upon the impression of 'true love' in providing orderly life and perfection. Here Jenny, a maid though not pure before her marriage, believes and respects her husband, for he makes her life joyous and endurable. She succeeds in winning her husband's 'loving-kindness' and tries to be his 'honest wife in heart and head from bride-ale hour to grave' :

Wedded they were. Her husband's trust
    In Jenny knew to bound,
And Jenny kept her pure and just,
Till even malice found

. . . .

She kissed him long, as when, just wooed,
She chose his domicile.
She felt she would give more than life
To be the single — hearted wife. (28)

The poet's portrayal of love which provides man 'life-loyalty' is, indeed, noteworthy. Hardy thinks that true love in reality is a spiritual awakening of man's creative life. Hardy's concept of noble love is comparable to Sri Aurobindo's : "Love is not love if it acquiesces in evil; great and true love is a power, and it can break the doors of captivity; it can change dross to gold, it can defy death or it is not love".[6] There are many love poems such as 'To Lizbie Browne' (PPP) 'To Louisa in the Lane' (WW) and '1967' (TL) which illustrate Hardy's gospel of love. Love, according to Hardy if justifiably pursued will bring joy, bliss, hope and inspiration to human existence. These lyrics throw light upon the question why man follows the path of love for his self-purification and realization. In the poem '1967' written a century earlier in 1867, Hardy asserts that love must be passionate and gracious. Such a mode of love with warmth which he calls 'loving-kindness' surely enriches the quality of man's life :

A century which, if not sublime,
Will show, I doubt not, at its prime,
A scope above this blinkered time.

— Yet what to me how far above?
For I would only ask thereof
That thy worm should be my worm, Love!

(167)

Just the same, 'Man-Society' relationship is shown as fruitful. Many of the Hardyan characters return to society, adjust and reconcile with their neighbours. They help others; love and respect the people around them; and sacrifice something for common betterment. In a similar spirit, they try to overcome their antipathies and follow a kind of ethic which Hardy calls 'Positive Religion'. In his view "*The Positive Religion* — contains the only laws capable of regulating the Present with a view to the Future on the basis of the Past."[7] In existentialism this doctrine is called 'stoic-resignation' or 'lucid-indifference' or 'life in meditation of isolation' which will eventually stabilize man's life even in case of society's indifference to an individual. This aspect of Hardy's ethic is reflected in 'Friends Beyond', 'Conjecture' and 'Wessex Heights'. Though it is a picture of dead people, the first poem shows how some people by nature are self-sacrificing. In this transitory or unreal world, William Dewy, Tranter Reuban, Farmer Ledlow, Squire and Lady Susan who lie in Mellstock (Stinsford) churchyard, sacrifice everything they had in a dramatic manner :

W.D. — 'Ye mid burn the old bass-viol that I set such value by'.

Squire — 'You may hold the manse in fee, You may wed my spouse, may let my children's memory of me die'.

Lady S. — 'You may have my rich brocades, my laces; take each household key;
Ransack coffer, desk, bureau;
Quiz the few poor treasures hid there,
con the letters kept by me. (36)

If the people of 'Friends Beyond' are fictional the people of Conjecture' are real and autobiographical. Here Hardy states if he had no Emma (his first wife), Florence (his second wife) and Mary (his sister), his life 'could pass to pulseless sleep!'

If there were in my kalendar
No Emma, Florence, Mary,
What would be my existence now —
A hermit's? — wanderer's weary? —
How should I live, and how
Near would be death, or far? (418)

In Hardy's view in the absence of the sunny atmosphere of his fellow beings, man cannot lead a happy life. But 'Wessex Heights' gives a contrasting picture as it shows the possibility of lonely life in isolation. Here the hero, disgraced from society alienates himself from it and lives happily on his favourite Wessex heights. His life like that of Robinson Crusoe's is in a state of physical isolation alone.

However, Hardy like existentialists, considers society a necessity for the possibility of human existence. He thinks human virtues harmonise all human relationships — 'sexual', 'personal' and 'social'

— and make them fruitful. A deep study of Hardyan metaphysics supports the fact that 'Love' can lead man to 'life-loyalties'. Admittedly Hardy advocates man to live with others in perfect harmony and he calls it 'scientific humanism' which is endorsed by existentialist thinkers. Naturally Jaspers remarks; "Remoteness from the world gives an inward distinction; but immersion, on the other hand, awakens all that is human in selfhood.... This historical immersion... is to be encountered in the energy of veneration, as concentration in occupational work, and as exclusivity in erotic love."[8] Sartre means the same when he says man should not live at the expense of others. As man's concept of freedom and responsibility involves others, others are indispensable to his existence. In Sartre's words if man is aware of the limit of his freedom, duty and responsibility, he will also be aware of others. Now the question is whether Hardyan protagonists follow the beaten track of tradition with a view to preserve their self and find perfection. But our study of Hardy supports the argument that his protagonists search new ways and means for the perfection of their lives instead of following the old track. Accordingly, though people inherit a tradition, they search a better order of life for fulfilment. They need a true bond of love and fellowship, truth, morals and creativity which are the traits of greatness. They aspire for purposive life. Indeed, they work for the attainment of rational, enlightened and progressive human evolution which can help them to become 'supermen'.

Under these circumstances, the Hardyan protagonist tries to establish a cordial human relationship with his fellow-beings. Here, Hardy speaks of man's return to society — of course, on a different level than that of an ordinary man. It is a return of an individual to society at the existentialist level as the authentic man who has encountered inwardness in solitude and longs for a communion with others. According to him, the authentic man joins the society in order to overcome his negative emotions and to recognise his own self. In support of this, he quotes Goethe: "*We first know that* we exist when we recognise ourselves in others."[9] In a similar note, Russian existentialist thinker, Berdyaev states; "The Ego longs to emerge from its prison house in order to meet and identify itself with another Ego."[10] Heidegger and Jaspers too state that for the realization of selfhood, man must establish a harmonious co-existence with his society. Jaspers thinks man's co-existence with society is 'Communication', while Buber does not accept Sartre's view of freedom saying his idea of freedom leads man to his (man's) mutual 'Cummunion'. He goes a step further and says that the possibility of 'Man and Man' contact facilitates the possibility of 'Man — Society' relationship. Here 'society' stands for the 'eternal presence' or 'real speech' as he called it. His idea of 'interpersonal relationship' is called 'Dialogue' which is similar to Jaspers' idea of 'communication' and Hardy's concept of 'social relationship'. According to this hypothesis, an individual and community are inter-dependent and one cannot live at the expense or exclusion of the other. So one's progress is wholly dependent on other'. It is true, social relationship (Dialogue) is necessary to man for his existence in relation to transcendence. Even, primal satisfaction comes to an individual with the establishment of a 'Dialogue' between him and society which, in fact, enables him to live in the world. The concept of 'Dialogue' provides a true foundation for an authentic mode of life in society. Kierkegaard believes that for man's salvation, his bond with the world must not be abandoned. In this regard, Buber criticises Sartre's idea of 'crowd' (society). He distinguishes the 'community' from the 'crowd' and tells that "Man's existence in the community is not bundled but bound."[11] He means man's relationship is not with the crowd, but with the systematic community, and man has nothing to do with society at large. It is true as our observation of life proves, man is only intimately bound to 'others' at a personal level without losing his individuality which carries him to the greater bondage with the community but not with the crowd. And this can only be done by man, a superior human being in the cosmos. This is supported by the traditional view that man is a rational and social animal who can mould his future according to his predetermined plans and projects. Here, the concern of both Hardy and existentialist thinkers is to know how individuals can establish an adequate interpersonal relationship with society as a preliminary to the attainment of perfection.

Again for the perfection of life, Hardyan protagonists do not follow any religion. They hardly turn either to religion or God for whatever psychic consolation and concrete help they may require. Even they deny the existence of supernatural forces. In their view the sanctity of religion is obliterated; and the transcendental bliss of it is no more extant. Now religion is not a spirit or force, but a farce. Therefore it has met with scathing criticism in the works of Hardy and existentialist thinkers. Indeed, "Religion, Whatever destinies my be in store for it, is at least for the present hardly any longer an organic power. It is not that supreme, penetrating, controlling, decisive part of a man's life."[12]

In many of Hardy's poems man's dislike for rituals, churches and clergy is vividly portrayed. His poems 'The Impercipient' and 'Unkept Good Fridays' show man's dislike for the religion-oriented way of life. In the first poem a man's loss of faith in the old way of life is delineated. The protagonist of it is unable to believe the things which his comrades do, for they seem to him mere fantasies. His blindness to see and inability to enjoy life are because of his loss of faith in the traditional mode of life based on religious absurdities. His loss of belief in Christianity is indicated by the imagery. The final image can 'a bird-deprived of wings go earth-bound wilfully!' denotes his atheism. He thinks that the world is dark so that his soul is 'consigned to infelicity'. Therefore, like Nietzsche, he thinks accepting Christianity is a 'self-deception', for no Christ breathes blessings :

> That He who breathes All's Well to these
> Breathes no All's — Well to me. (44)

The poem also reflects Hardy's autobiographical elements. Hardy's second wife Mrs. Florence Emily Hardy says that Hardy lost his faith in Christianity by the age of 27. He considered the so called morality as the very cause of man's suffering which he termed as 'positive evil'. He wrote "Unless *suffering* is the direct and immediate object of life, our *existence* must entirely fail of its aim"... "happiness of any given life is to be measured, not by its joys and pleasures, but by the extent to which it has been free from suffering from positive evil".[13] Hardy was angry with the dogmatic clergy who defended the evils of religion. L.E.W. Smith rightly remarks; "...What distressed Hardy even more, and this perhaps implies a failure of faith in the 'believers', is their lack of 'Sympathies and Christian charity."[14] As a result, he was accused of being a pessimist, fatalist and non-conformist as Socrates was charged with being Godless and corrupting the youth of Athens. But Hardy was not what people thought of him. In fact, he did not wish to do anything without Christian charity and loving-kindness. L.E.W. Smith again remarks; "If there were true Christians they would sympathise with his 'lack' and 'shortcomings' : they could act out of strength, optimism and faith, but yet they accused him."[14] For example in the poem in spite of weakness and deprivation, the agnostic man is ready to act with sympathy and love in quest of becoming himself. Therefore, he proclaims :

Enough, As yet disquiet clings
About us. Rest shall we, (44)

In the other poem 'Unkept Good Fridays' written on the Good Friday of 1927, Hardy criticises the glorious celebration of *Good Fridays*. He thinks there are many more Good Fridays of men who were slain for the goodwill of kings and whose Good Fridays are not observed. However, as the traditional way of life exploits the poor and degenerates the rich, he thinks it is not worth celebrating these nameless Christ's Good Fridays. Hardy also criticises the clergy and the churches in the poems, 'She Revisits Alone the Church of Her Marriage' (LLE) and 'The Levelled Churchyard' (PPP). Here Hardyan protagonists animated by heroic qualities rebel against the clergy and the absurd religious institutions which curb he man's freedom and responsibility. Whatever they want to do they resolve to do it independently without any assistance from the established religious institutions or from any incomprehensible forces. Because they are self-reliant, conscious and hardworking so they seek consolation and contentment only in their fellow-beings or in their biological environment.

Existentialist thinkers have also criticised the adverse impact of religion, rituals, churches and the clergy. Sartre has considered religion a bundle of superstitious beliefs, while Kierkegaard affirms; "It must be irrational to become a christian", and "to become a christian is to risk everything, to invest absolutely everything in the venture."[15] Here one thing should be remembered that Hardy has never denied the benevolence and significance of the true spirit of religion which lies in faith, charity, sacrifice, forgiveness and loving-kindness. But he does not believe in artificial rites and rituals. Besides, Hardyan protagonists do not believe in the existence and benevolence of God. In their view God is not a force to deliver them power and glory. This aspect of Hardyan protagonists' agnosticism and atheism is clearly reflected in poems like 'Hap', 'The Bedridden Peasant' and 'New Year's Eve'. These poems disclose man's fight against God for his progressive enlightenment. The sonnct 'Hap' denotes how God personified as 'Crass Casualty', 'dicing Time' and 'purblind Doomsters' readily frustrates human desires and endeavours :

— Crass Casualty obstructs the sun and rain,
And dicing Time for gladness casts a moan....
These purblind Doomsters had as readily strown
Blisses about my pilgrimage as pain. (4)

'The Bedridden Peasant' sub-titled *To an unknowing God* establishes God's indifference and irresponsibility. Here the protagonist thinks that God is not only neutral but also indifferent to mankind. Therefore, he declares :

Much wonder I — here long low — laid —
 That this dead wall should be
Betwixt the Maker and the made,
 Between Thyself and me! (88)

A close observation of Hardy's poem 'New Year's Eve' in which the victim asks God for his gracious presence, expresses the protagonist's bitter comment on God. The poem attracted many readers and critics alike, for God in the poem is shown as unanswerable to the question why he created man and left him in 'tabernacle groan'. He is shown as a sense-sealed power caring only for the process of Nature which is also indifferent to human existence :

'I HAVE finished another year', said God,
 'In grey, green, white, and brown;
I have strewn the leaf upon the sod,
Sealed up the worm within the cold,
 And let the last sun down'.

'And what's the good of it?' I said,
 'What reasons made you call
From formless void this earth we tread,
When nine-and-ninety can be read
 Why nought should be at all?

'Yea, Sire; why shaped you us, "who in
 This tabernacle groan" —
If ever a joy be found herein,
Such joy no man had wished to win
 If he had never known!'

Then he : 'My labours-logicless-
 You may explain; not I :
Sense-sealed I have wrought, without a guess
That I evolved a Consciousness
 To ask for reasons why,

'Strange that ephemeral creatures who
 By my own ordering are,

Should see the shortness of my view,
Use ethic tests I never knew,
Or made provision for!'

He sank to raptness as of yore,
And opening New Year's Day
Wove it by rote as theretofore,
And went on working evermore
In his unweeting way. (231)

These poems show Hardy's views about the dark aspect of human existence which is overshadowed by the image of Godhead working blindly without any logic. Therefore Hardy's atheism is evident in his novels and short stories. It is because of Hardy's disbelief in Providence, his friend Edmund Gosse wrote; "What has Providence done to Mr. Hardy that he should rise up in the arable land of Wessex and shake his fist at his Creator?"[16] Hardy seems to have answered Gosse in the following unpublished poem :

The Gods...
Many things they have given and taken
And wrought and ruined many things......

Therefore, man should not depend either on religion or God for any concrete help; instead he has to be confident, courageous and hardworking. Similarly, he should create his own moral and social order of life. Indeed, "Those who no longer place their highest faith in powers above and beyond men, are for that very reason more deeply interested than others in cherishing the integrity, and worthiness of man himself."[17]

The existentialist thinker's criticism of God is still severe. Nietzsche heralds His death, while Sartre denies His existence as he insistently disbelieves Him. Still there are people who think that though God exists no ethical principles can be deduced from His existence. Hardy thinks; "If this (the doctrine of mere probability) were to be allowed then the celebrated saying "O God if there be a God, save my soul if I have a soul would be the highest measure of devotion ! : but who can really pray to a Being about whose existence he is seriously in doubt?"[18] It is true, an external force promising peace, prosperity, consolation and salvation is an illusion to curb one's feelings and courage. Admittedly man's ardent faith in God sickens him and destroys his very sense of freedom and responsibility without diminishing his misery and suffering. A note made in his diary on December 31,

1885 underlines Hardy's valuable advice to human beings; "This is the chief thing; be not perturbed; for all things are according to the nature of the universal (Marcus Aurelius)."[19]

No wonder, on account of his atheism, Hardy is harshly criticised. G.K. Chesterton (1874-1936) called him 'a village atheist'; Oxford university delayed to honour him; and many copies of his novel *Jude the Obscure* were burnt in public. It is true that Hardy is an atheist and an evolutionary meliorist. But a close glance at his poetry reveals that he also believes in an incomprehensible power that directs the world to a mysterious end, and is rather utterly indifferent to the human endeavours. However, with his atheism goes the belief that man is necessarily alone and he must work out his own destiny. An unsigned reviewer in *The Academy* wrote about Hardy that "The ordinary agnostic who has serious thought for his fellows offers a hard materialism in the place of the religion in which he finds no solace. Mr. Hardy, who is not ordinary, might be called an unbelieving mystic."[20]

Both Hardy and existentialist thinkers come to the conclusion that man does not inherit any values and his existence precedes essence. Accordingly, God is an essence created by ignorant people after they had gained existence. It is right man first exists and then only he hurls himself towards a future. At first he is nothing, it is only afterwards he achieves everything by his solidarity. Hence, both Hardy and existentialists arrive at a similar conclusion that man has to be conscious, heroic, hard-working and responsible for the purpose of self-realization in the purposeless universe. As nobody either guides or helps him, he has to attain whatever he needs by his own choice, action and responsibility. There is neither heaven nor hell to grant man either salvation or damnation. There is only one reality i.e., the world, the man and his consciousness. In such a reality man is his own God. Nevertheless, Hardy regrets that there are some orthodox people who believe in a nether world with a hope of getting a happy life after their death. For those people Hardy has a characteristic retort; " 'Do you know what it is which makes man the most suffering of creatures? It is that he has one foot in the finite and the other in the infinite.' "[21] Therefore, Hardyan protagonists denounce Godhead which is the root cause of their 'sickness unto death' (Kierkegaard). They disbelieve in the benevolence of religion-oriented traditional way of life which merely weakens human solidarity. Hardy's heroes are atheists and transcendentalists. Albeit, after reconsidering their situation once they have alienated themselves from the biological environment and material world, they reconcile and readjust to them with the hope of finding a better relationship of co-existence. Their compromise with the biological world and society overcomes their solitary confinement, dread and a feeling of nothingness. Furthermore, it generates in them a desire for collective life, but 'in identity of their distinct individuality'. In this connection they rebel against the convention and God only to recreate a new moral and social order of life. Indeed, they try to make human existence more endurable for the glorification of their earthly evolution.

REFERENCES

1. E.R. Oxford, 'Nature and Man', *Quarterly Lankaster*, p. 10.
2. D.R. Bhandari, *Darshana*, Vol. XXX, No. 2, p. 35.
3. W.H. Auden, 'A Literary Transference' ed. by A.J. Guerard, *Hardy : A Collection of Critical Essays*, p. 139.
4. Jean Brooks, 'The Homeliest of Heart — Stirings : Shorter Lyrics', ed. by James Gibson and Trevor Johnson, *Thomas Hardy Poems*, p. 209.
5. Ernest Brennecke, *The Life of Thomas Hardy*, p. 136.
6. Shri Aurobindo, qt. by K.R.S. Iyengar, *Indian Writing in English*, pp. 153-154.
7. Thomas Hardy, *Literary Notes I*, p. 74.
8. Karl Jaspers, *Man in the Modern Age*, tr. by Eden and Cedar Paul, p. 184.
9. Goethe, qt. by Thomas Hardy, *Literary Notes I*, p. 14.
10. Nikolai Berdyaev, qt. by Lakshmi Saxena, *Encounter with Transcendence*, p. 131.
11. Martin Buber, *The Knowledge of Man*, tr. by M. Friedman and R.G. Smith, p. 84.
12. John Morley, qt. by Thomas Hardy, *Literary Notes II*, p. 123.
13. Thomas Hardy, *Literary Notes II*, p. 28.
14. L.E.W. Smith, 'The Impercipient' ed. by James Gibson and Trevor Johnson, *Thomas Hardy Poems*, p. 189.
15. Kierkegaard, printed in 'Philosophy and Phenomenological Research', ed. by Ernest Sosa *A Quarterly Journal*, Vol. II, No. 2, pp. 301-302.
16. Edmund Gosse, qt. by Lois Deacon and Terry Coleman, *Providence and Mr. Hardy*, p. 7.
17. John Morley, qt. by Thomas Hardy, *Literary Notes II*, p. 122.
18. Thomas Hardy, *Literary Notes I*, p. 5.
19. *Life*, p. 176.
20. *The Academy*, p. 48.
21. Thomas Hardy, *Literary Notes I*, p. 128.

Conclusion

A keen study of Thomas Hardy's poetry displays that his poetry develops the tenets of existentialism. Though Hardy had not heard the term existentialism, as a sensitive poet he was able to capture the spirit of existentialism which was very much in the air during his life time. In this sense, Hardy is a modern writer though he was born and brought up during the 19th century. In most of his creative writing he is preoccupied with the theme of alienation and search for identity. Hardy's poetry depicts vividly how the conditions of life lead an individual to a state of isolation on the biological, social and personal levels.

Though Hardy does not condemn the advance of science and technology, he possesses a greater love and veneration for the pre-scientific world where man and Nature co-existed in harmonious relationship. Hardy's Nature poems written before he came under the impact of new faith, exclusively show the healthy attachment between man and Nature. Against this background, man lives in perfect harmony with natural environment and feels a sense of spiritual togetherness. However, with the advancement of science, the evils such as mechanization and materialism change man's attitude towards his surrounding. He separates himself from Nature with a view to control her for his material prosperity and comfort which modern science promise him. Man's estrangement from Nature is not just a result of his life in cities but one of a drastic change in his outlook towards Nature.

Hardy's approach to Nature is characterized by change in keeping with his emotional attitudes. Earlier he believed that Nature provided man spiritual satisfaction. He thought that those who saw Nature with love and veneration as conscious being, would surely feel an elevation of the spirit. Therefore, according to Hardy man must consider Nature his companion in order to ease his mental tensions. The importance that Hardy attaches to harmonious relationship between Man and Nature, aligns him with the theistic existentialist thinkers. Like the theistic existentialist thinker Karl Jaspers, Hardy advocates an 'I-Thou' relationship between man and Nature. Hardy's predilection to view Nature with a spiritual eye and not merely through the physical eye is significant. His advice to man as it is conveyed through his protagonists is that man should choose an attitude of love, sympathy, friendship and veneration towards Nature. If man approaches Nature with such attitude, according to Hardy, he will be blessed with spiritual comfort, joy, consolation and contentment. Hardy thinks the adverse impact of industrialization and scientism frustrates man's desires to establish a healthy relationship with his natural milieu.

Hardy emphasizes the alienation of man from society, when he finds a disruption both in familial and community life. This is because of the conflict caused between an individual and community. Man's ambition, greed and enmity counteract his desire to attain fulfilment in family life. As a result, when man tries to be happy in society, the society which does not care for life-generating values, hinders the path of progress of an individual. This makes the individual a powerless entity in the increasingly complex world. Subsequently, an individual who is in quest of selfhood alienates from society. This aspect of human existence is depicted in Hardy's poems 'Wessex Heights', and 'In Tenebris' I, II and III.

Hardy fought throughout his life against cruelty to living beings both big and small, human beings and animals. He declares that what he wrote is nothing, but 'one plea against man's inhumanity to man, woman and lower creatures'. He criticises society for its inhuman treatment of individuals. According to Hardy a healthy society is neither moral, nor immoral but amoral. Like the existentialist thinkers Kierkegaard and Sartre who condemn the power of the multitude or society which smothers all that is authentic, beautiful and individualistic, Hardy is extremely critical of the crowd as a threat to individual liberty. He depicts vividly the terror an individual feels for the crowd in many of his poems. In a sense, Hardy's work foreshadows Franz Kafka's novel *The Trial.* The hero of Kafka's novel, Joseph K is exploited by the masses in the name of justice, and he becomes a victim of social disorders.

The depressing conditions of human existence lead man to a state of self-alienation. The disparity between what man aspires to become and what he can do, causes a serious threat to the integrity of his selfhood. Hardy depicts this aspect of human life through his characters in the poems 'Wessex Heights', 'The Milk Maid' and the three poems of the Latin name 'In Tenebris'. The philosophy of existentialism considers self-alienation as a grave condition of modern man.

Self-alienation which is a major theme in modern psychology, is a tragic phenomenon in Hardy's poems. As many of Hardy's people who neither desire to admit defeat nor wish to commit suicide, remain in a state of mental tumult and moral tensions. Such conditions may make many wish to put an end to life; induce some to decide to defy society even at the cost of their lives; but incite only a few to withstand the trials and tribulations and succeed in life.

It has been noticed that Hardy does not approve the idea of suicide because it proves man's inherent cowardice. Of course the protagonists of his poems 'Wessex Heights' and 'In Tenebris' do not desire to live in society, they alienate themselves from it and live in solitude. With their principle of stoic-resignation and inner resources, they harmonise their lives in order to achieve transcendental bliss. In fact, they succeed in their quest for selfhood even in the face of glaring misfortunes. Hardy's humanism is evident in his men and women who despite their separation from their homeland Nature and human solidarity, find a code of conduct that amply ensures them contentment. True the way, his protagonists pursue peace, prosperity, health and happiness leads them to 'life-loyalty'.

Hardy's disbelief in Christian faith stems from the assumption that Christianity is full of dogmas and rituals which are outdated, meaningless and harmful. According to Hardy, religion is degenerated. He also thinks God is indifferent to man. For example, Hardy's protagonists portrayed in 'Hap', 'The Bedridden Peasant' and 'New Year's Eve' are deeply troubled when their endeavours are thwarted by some unknown powers which Hardy names as God, Crass Casualty, Fate, Destiny, Immanent Will and so on. Hardy's scathing criticism of religion and God has its counterpart in the philosophy of existence. Kierkegaard, the founder of existentialism has criticized the notions of Christian charity and loving-kindness, while Nietzsche has announced the death of God. Sartre declares even if God exists no ethical principles could be deduced from his existence as man and God pass each other by without touching. According to these thinkers religion and God curtail man's freedom and discourage him from action and responsibility. They fail to satisfy his thirst for peace and consolation.

When all means of transcendence such as Nature, Society or the loved ones become useless, Hardy thinks man can take recourse only to his self which in the absence of God and any aid from outside, can provide him choice and responsibilities. Hardy blames God for His indifference towards human misery and suffering. As it has already been noted in the poem 'Hap' God does not help man in his hours of crisis. Therefore, Hardy does not believe in God's benevolence. Indeed, it is a form of revolt against God.

Hardy does not consider man an insignificant entity in the world which is alien to him. He considers man a conscious entity who can live independently without any assistance from forces beyond himself. Hardy commands our attention, because through his tragic protagonists he portrays human existence — an existence in which man alienates himself from Nature, from society and from his own self. His depiction of life as reflected in his poems shows an important phenomenon of human existence that is 'man is made to live, and he is called to die, and life offers to deny!' He considers pain, suffering and death as characteristic features of human life. In this regard, man's self-alienation is not a grave danger to his self-realization because self-alienation leads to self-examination which in turn gives him a better perspective of his existence. Man's desire to attain the status which he best deserves, can be fulfilled by his right choice, heroic action and responsibility. He can achieve his good, *viz.* his selfhood if his relationship harmonizes with his biological environment, society and his own inner self. He believes in man's right conscience which, according to him, enables everyone to choose rightly and act accordingly. He thinks that whatever man does — whether he helps or harms, pleases or teases or does anything at all depends upon his self-awareness. In fact self-consciousness is very important for man's commitments. In addition to this, Hardy thinks courage and confidence are necessary to man for his attainment of self-hood. He questions how a man who is not courageous enough can dare and act in a worthwhile manner in life. In fact, in Hardy's vision of life, man must possess enquiring spirit, courage, confidence, determination and dedication. In a similar spirit, Hardy believes in action too. Like Sartre, Hardy thinks man is a sum total and grand result of his actions. He will be what he dares and does. In his view actions that are meaningful find an important place in life. As Ortega Y Gasset thinks a book is made of pages,

Hardy thinks life is made of actions and situations. In existentialism man's character is said to evolve from the way he acts and responds to the situations of his life.

Thus, in Hardy's scheme of things man is a significant entity in the universe. He can attain whatever he desires by sheer dint of right choice, action and responsibility. In fact, he can attain transcendental bliss if he lives in perfect harmony with his biological environment, material world and inner self. Hardy believed in the gradual evolution of man. In his poems he depicts how man alienates himself from Nature, Society and Himself because of his critical attitude towards life. After an analysis of his relationship with Nature, Society and Himself, he realizes the possibility of a new adjustment in the light of the knowledge he has gained in the process. At the end of this experience, he finds himself better because he has come to transcend his individual limitations. In this sense, Hardyan characters come nearer to the Nietzschian idea of superman.

A Select Bibliography

I. THOMAS HARDY'S WORKS

(A) POETRY

Wessex Poems and Other Verses (1898), London : Harper and Brothers, 1898.

Poems of the Past and the Present (1902), London : Harper and Brothers, 1902.

Time's Laughingstocks and Other Verses (1909), London : Macmillan and Co., 1909.

Satires of Circumstance, Lyrics and Reveries (1914), London : Macmillan and Co., 1914.

Moments of Vision and Miscellaneous Verses (1917), London : Macmillan and Co., 1917.

Late Lyrics and Earlier (1922), London : Macmillan and Co., 1922.

Human Shows, Far Phantasies : Songs and Trifles (1925), London : Macmillan and Co., 1925.

Winter Words in Various Moods and Metres (1928), London : Macmillan and Co., 1928.

The Complete Poems, ed. James Gibson, London : Macmillan and Co. Ltd., 1976.

(B) FICTION

Desperate Remedies (1871), London : Macmillan and Co. Ltd., 1953.

Under the Greenwood Tree (1872), New York : St. Martin's Press, 1966.

A Pair of Blue Eyes (1873), London : Macmillan and Co. Ltd., 1975.

Far from the Madding Crowd (1874), London : Macmillan and Co. Ltd., 1969.

The Hand of Ethelberta (1875), London : Macmillan and Co. Ltd., 1951.

The Return of the Native (1876-'78), New York : Harper and Row Publishers, 1922.

The Trumpet Major (1878-'80), London : Macmillan and Co. Ltd., 1967.

A Laodicean (1880-'81), London : Macmillan and Co. Ltd., 1975.

Two on a Tower (1882), London : Macmillan and Co. Ltd., 1949.

The Mayor of Casterbridge (1886), USA : Dell Publishing Co., 1970.

The Woodlanders (1887), New York : Macmillan, St. Martin Press, 1967.

Tess of the D'Urbervilles (1891), USA : Dell Publishing Co., 1970.

Jude the Obscure (1895), London : Macmillan and Co. Ltd., 1951, and New York : A Signet Classic, 1961.

The Well-Beloved (1897), London : Macmillan and Co., Ltd., 1952.

(C) SHORT-STORIES

A Changed Man (1913), London : Macmillan and Co. Ltd., 1927.

A Group of Noble Dames (1891), London : J.R. Osgood, McIlvaine and Co., 1891.

Life's Little Ironies (1894), London : Macmillan and Co. Ltd., 1953.

Wessex Tales (1888), London : Macmillan and Co. Ltd., 1888.

(D) DRAMA

The Dynasts, London : Macmillan and Co. Ltd., Part I, 1903 : Part II, 1906; Part III, 1908.

The Famous Tragedy of the Queen of Cornwall (1923).

II. STUDIES ON THOMAS HARDY

Abercrombie, Lascelles, *Thomas Hardy : A Critical Study*, London : Martin Secker Ltd., 1935.

Bayley, John, *An Essay on Hardy*, New York : CUP, 1978.

Bjork. L.A. (ed.), *The Literary Notebooks of Thomas Hardy* Vol. I and II, London : Macmillan and Co. Ltd., 1985.

Blunden, Edmund, *Thomas Hardy*, London : Macmillan and Co. Ltd., 1942.

Boumelha, Penny, *Thomas Hardy and Woman, Sexual Ideology and Narrative Form*, Sussex; The Harvester Press, 1982.

Brennecke, Ernest. Jr., *The Life of Thomas Hardy,* New York : Greenberg Publishers, Inc., 1925.

Broades, E.K. and Gordon, R.K. (Sel. and ed.), *English Prose from Bacon to Hardy*, London : OUP., 1918.

Brooks, Jean. R., *Thomas Hardy : The Poetic Structure*, London : Elek Press, 1971.

Brown, Douglas, *Thomas Hardy*, London : Longmans, 1961.

Butler, Lance St. John, *Thomas Hardy : After Fifty Years*, London : The Macmillan Press Ltd., 1977.

Butler, Lance St. John, *Thomas Hardy*, Cambridge : CUP, 1978.

Carpenter, Richard, *Thomas Hardy*, London : The Macmillan Press Ltd., 1976.

Cecil, David, *Hardy : The Novelist*, London : Constable and Co. Ltd., 1943.

Chew, Samuel C., *Thomas Hardy : Poet and Novelist*, New York : Alfred Aknapf Press, 1928.

Child, Harold, *Thomas Hardy*, London : Nisbet and Co. Ltd. 1916.

Cox, R.G. (ed.), *Thomas Hardy : The Critical Heritage*, London : Reutledge and Kegan Paul Ltd., 1970.

Davie, Donald, *Thomas Hardy and British Poetry*, London : Routledge and Kegan Paul, 1973.

Deacon, Lois and Coleman, Terry, *Providence and Mr. Hardy*, London : Hutchinson and Co. Ltd., 1966.

D'exideuil, Pierre, *The Human Pair in the Works of Thomas Hardy*, London : Humphrey Toulmin Press, 1930.

Draper, R.P. (ed.), *Thomas Hardy : Three Pastoral Novels*, London : Macmillan Education Ltd., 1987.

Duffin, H.C., *Thomas Hardy*, Manchester : MUP, 1962.

Enstice, Andrew, *Thomas Hardy : Landscape of the Mind*, London : The Macmillan Press Ltd., 1979.

Furbank, P.N. (ed.), *Selected Poems of Thomas Hardy,* London : Macmillan and Co. Ltd., 1964.

Gibson, James and Johnson, Trever (ed.), *A Selection of Critical Essays on Thomas Hardy Poems*, London : The Macmillan Press Ltd., 1979.

Gregor, Ian, *The Great Web*, London : Faber and Faber, 1974.

Grundy, Joan, *Hardy and the Sister Arts*, London : Macmillan Press Ltd., 1979.

Guerard, A.J. (ed.), *Hardy : A Collection of Critical Essays*, Englewood Cliffs, N.J : Prentice Hall Inc., 1963.

Hardy, Evelyn, *Thomas Hardy's Notebooks*, London : The Hogarth Press, 1955.

Hardy, F.E., *The Early Life of Thomas Hardy* (1840-1891), London : Macmillan and Co. Ltd., 1928.

Hardy, F.E., *The Later Years of Thomas Hardy* (1892-1928), London : Macmillan and Co. Ltd., 1930.

Hasan, Noorul, *Thomas Hardy : The Sociological Imagination*, Delhi : Macmillan Indian Ltd., 1982.

Hawkins, Desmond, *Thomas Hardy*, London : Arthur Barker Ltd., 1950.

Holland, Clive, *Thomas Hardy, OM The Man His Works and the Land of Wessex*, London : Herbert Jenkins Ltd., 1933.

Johnson, Lionel, *The Art of Thomas Hardy*, London : The Macmillan Press Ltd., 1892.

Johnson, Trevor, *Thomas Hardy*, New York : Arco Publishing Co. Inc., 1971.

Lea, Hermann, *Thomas Hardy's Wessex*, London : Macmillan and Co., Ltd., 1925.

Leeson, Edward (ed.), *The Bedside Thomas Hardy*, London : Macmillan Co. Ltd., 1979.

Marsdon, Kenneth, *The Poems of Thomas Hardy*, London : The Macmillan Press Ltd., 1967.

McDowall, Arthur, *Thomas Hardy : A Critical Study*, London : Faber and Faber Ltd., 1953.

Meisel, Perry, *Thomas Hardy : The Return of the Repressed*, London : Yale Univ. Press, 1972.

Miller, J.H., *Thomas Hardy : Distance and Desire,* Cambridge : The Belknap Press, 1970.

Millgate, Michael, *Thomas Hardy : His Career as a Novelist*, London : The Bodley Head, 1971.

Morel, R., *Thomas Hardy : The Will and the Way*, Malaya : OUP, 1965.

Orel, Harold, *Thomas Hardy's Personal Writings*, London : Macmillan Press Ltd., 1967.

Page, Norman, *Thomas Hardy*, London : Routledge and Kegan Paul, 1977.

Patil, Dr. Mallikarjun, *Thomas Hardy : The Poet : A Critical Study*, New Delhi : Atlantic Publishers and Distributors, 1997.

Paulin, Tom, *Thomas Hardy : The Poetry of Perception*, London : The Macmillan Ltd., 1975.

Pinion, F.B., *A Hardy Companion*, London : Macmillan Ltd., 1968.

Puk, Francine Shapiro (ed.), *Thomas Hardy's Chosen Poems*, New York Frederick Unger Publishing Co., 1978.

Ranjankumar, *Thomas Hardy : A Study of his concept of Nature*, Delhi : Classical Publication, 1990.

Rutland, William R., *Thomas Hardy : A Study of His Writings and Their Background*, Oxford : Basil Blackwell, 1938.

Rutland, W.R., *Thomas Hardy*, London : Blackie and Sons Ltd., 1938.

Salter, C.H., *Good Little Thomas Hardy*, London : The Macmillan Press Ltd., 1981.

Scott, James, R.A., *Thomas Hardy*, London : The British Council and the National Book League, Longman, 1951.

Southerington, F.R., *Hardy's Vision of Man*, London : Chatto and Windus, 1971.

Southworth, J.G., *The Poetry of Thomas Hardy*, New York : Columbia Univ. Press, 1947.

Stewart, J.I.M., *Thomas Hardy* : A Critical Biography, London : Longman, 1971.

Sumner, Rosemary, *Thomas Hardy : Psychological Novelist*, London : The Macmillan Ltd., 1981.

Taylor, Dennis, *Hardy's Poetry*, London : The Macmillan Press Ltd., 1981.

Tylor Richard, H., *The Personal Notebooks of Thomas Hardy*, London : The Macmillan Press Ltd., 1979.

Wain, John, *Selected Stories of Thomas Hardy*, London : Macmillan Press Ltd., 1966.

Weber, Carl. J., *Hardy of Wessex*, Columbia : Col. Univ. Press, 1940.

Webster, H.C., *On a Darkling Plain*, Chicago : The Univ. of Chicago Press, 1947.

Whitefield, A. Stanton, *Thomas Hardy : The Artist and the Disciple of Destiny*, London : Grant Richards Ltd., 1921.

White, R.J., *Thomas Hardy and History*, London : The Macmillan Press Ltd., 1974.

Widenfield, Howe. I., and Nicholson, *Thomas Hardy*, London : Macmillan Press Ltd., 1963.

Williams, Merryn, *A Preface to Hardy*, New York : Longman, 1976.

III. ESSAYS AND ARTICLES ON THOMAS HARDY

Collins, V.H., "The Love Poetry of Thomas Hardy" rpt. *Essays and Studies*, collected by R.W. Chapman, Vol. XXVIII, 1942, Oxford : Clarendon Press, 1943.

Galli, Christopher, *Movements in English Literature*, Cambridge : CUP, 1975.

Gifford, Henry, "An Essay on Hardy and Emma", rpt. *Essays and Studies*, edited by R.M. Wilson, London : John Murry Press, 1966.

Lucas, F.L., "Hardy" rpt., *Eight Victorian Poets,* Cambridge : CUP, 1930.

Quiller Couch, Sir Arthur, "The Poetry of Thomas Hardy", rpt., *Studies in Literature*, Cambridge : CUP, 1919.

Thomas, Henry and Thomas, Dana Lee, *Famous Novelists,* New York : Blue Ribben Books, 1946.

IV. PHILOSOPHICAL AND RELATED STUDIES

Allen, E.L., *Existentialism From Within*, London : Routledge and Kegan Paul, 1953.

Blackham, H.J., *Six Existenialist Thinkers*, London : Routledge and Kegan Paul Ltd., 1952.

Bretall, Robert (ed.), *A Kierkegaard Anthology*, New York : Princeton Univ. Press, 1947.

Buber, Martin, *The Knowledge of Man*, translated by M. Friedman and R.G. Smith, London : George Allen and Unwin Press, 1965.

Camus, Albert, *The Rebel*, tr. Anthony Bower, Harmondsworth : Penguin Books, 1984.

Chatterjee, Margaret, *The Existential Outlook*, Bombay : Orient Longman, 1973.

Copleston, S.J. Frederick, *A History of Philosophy*, Vol. 7, Part II, New York : A Division of Double Day and Co. Inc., 1965.

Eric and Mary, Josephson, *Man Alone Alienation in Modern Society*, New York : Dell Laurel edition, 1962.

Foulquie, Faul, *Existentialism*, translated by Raine Kathleen, London : Dennis Dobson Ltd., 1947.

Heidegger, Martin, *Being and Time*, translated by John Macquarrie, London : S.C.M. Press, 1962.

Heidegger, Martin, *Existence and Being*, translated by Brock, London : Vision Press, 1919.

Husserl, Edmund, *Ideas : General Introduction to Pure Phenomenology* tr. W.R. Royce, London : George Allen and Unwin Ltd., 1958.

Jaspers, Karl, *Man in the Modern Age*, translated by Eden and Cidar Paul, London : Routledge and Kegan Pul Ltd., 1951.

Jaspers, Karl, *Philosophical Faith and Revelation*, translated by E.B. Ashaton Collins, London : St. James Place, 1967.

Jaspers, Karl, *Reason and Existence* (ed.), William Earle, New York : Straus Farrar, 1960.

Kant, Immanuel, *Critique of Pure Reason*, translated by Max Mueller, New York : Macmillan, 1925.

Kaufman, Walter, *The Portable Nietzsche*, New York : The Viking Press, 1954.

Kierkegaard, Soren, *Concluding Unscientific Postscript*, translated by D.F. Swenson and W. Lowrie, Princeton : PUP, 1949.

Kumar, Basant, *Contemporary Indian Philosophy*, Delhi : Motilal Banarsidas Press, 1973.

Lewis, H.D., *The Elusive Mind*, London : George Allen and Unwin Ltd., 1969.

Lutoslavaski, W., *Pre-Existence and Reincarnation,* London : George Allen and Unwin Ltd., 1928.

Macquarrie, John, *Existentialism*, Harmondsworth : Penguin Book, 1972.

Mann, Heinrich, *The Living Thoughts of Nietzsche,* London : Cassell and Co. Ltd., 1939.

Mounier, Emmanuel, *Existential Philosophies*, London : Rockliff, Salisbury, Square, 1948.

Nietzsche, F., *The Gay Science*, translated by Walter Kaufman, New York : Untage Books Random House, 1974.

Parker, D.H., *Human Values*, New York : Harper and Brother, 1931.

Radhakrishnan, S., *Indian Philosophy*, London : Allen and Unwin Ltd., 1951.

Russel, Burtrand, *Western Philosophies*, London : George Allen and Unwin Ltd., 1946.

Sartre, J.P., *Existentialism,* translated by Bernard Frenchtman, London : Rider and Co., Hutchinson House, 1955.

Sartre, J.P., *Being and Nothingness*, translated by Hazel, E. Barnes, New York : Washington Square Press, 1966.

Sartre, J.P., *Nausea*, translated by L. Alexander, London : Hamish Hamilton, 1962.

Saxena, Laxmi, *Encounter with Transcendence,* Delhi : G.D.K. Publications, 1983.

Schopenhauer, Arthur, *The World as Will and Idea*, Book IV, Vol. I, London : Kegan Paul and Co. Ltd., 1896.

Schrader, George Alfred Jr., (ed.), *Existential Philosophers : Kierkegaard to Merleau Ponty*, New York : MacGrow Hill Book Co., 1967.

Sharma, L.P., *History of Madieval India*, Delhi : K.P. Pvt. Ltd., 1982.

Sherburne, Donald W., *A Key of Whitehead's Process and Reality*, New York : Macmillan Co. Ltd., 1966.

Sinari, R.A., *Contemporary Existentialism-its Limitations*, Bombay, BUP, 1958.

Solomon, Robert, C., *From Rationalism to Existentialism,* USA : Humanities Press, 1978.

Srinivasan, G., *The Existential Concepts and The Hindu Philosophical System*, Allahabad : Udayana Publication, 1967.

Srinivasan, G., *Personalism,* Delhi : Research Publication, 1972.

Srinivasan G., *Philosophical Perspectives : East and West*, Mysore : Associated Printers, 1988.

Srinivasan G., *The Self and its Ideals in East-West Philosophy*, Trivendrum : College Book House, 1974.

Talapatra, Asha, *A Critical Study of Sartre's Plays as Literature and as Theatre*, Bombay : BUP, 1985.

Thilly, Frank, *History of Philosophies*, Allahabad : I.V. Press, 1976.

Thomas and Thomas, *Religious Leaders*, Bombay Bharatiya Vidya Bhavan, 1955.

Wahl, Jean, *Philosophy of Existence*, translated by F.M. Lory, London : Routledge and Kegan Paul, 1969.

Wagner, Warren (ed.), *Science, Faith and Man-European Thought Since, 1914*, London : Macmillan and Co. Ltd., 1968.

Warnock, Mary, *The Philosophy of Sartre*, London : Hutchinson Press, 1965.

Whitehead, A.N., *The Function of Reason*, Boston : Beacon Press Beacon, 1962.

Whitehead, A.N. *Process and Reality*, Cambridge : CUP, 1929.

V. ESSAYS AND ARTICLES ON EXISTENTIALISM

A Quarterly Journal, Vol. LI, No. 2, edited by Ernest Sosa, Ann Arber : Michigan : Braun Brumfield Inc. June 1991.

Darshana : An International Quarterly of Philosophy, edited by D.R. Bhandari, Vol. XXX, Moradabad : April 1990.

International Philosophical Quarterly, edited by Vincent G. Potter, S.J., New York : March 1991.

Quarterly Lankaster, edited by E.R. Oxford, London : 1905.

The Encyclopedia of Philosophy, Vol. IV, edited by Paul Edwards, New York : Macmillan Publishing Co. Inc., 1967.

INDEX